The Travel Diary of a Modern-day British

Adventurer During the 2021 Taliban Takeover

LORD MILES

IN AFGHANISTAN

— LORD MILES ROUTLEDGE —

ANTELOPE HILL PUBLISHING

Cover art by Swifty.
Literary development by Taylor Young.
Edited and formatted by Margaret Bauer.

Antelope Hill Publishing
www.antelopehillpublishing.com

Paperback ISBN-13: 978-1-956887-53-2
EPUB ISBN-13: 978-1-956887-54-9

Contents

May 5th
The Embassy

HERE IT IS, I THOUGHT TO MYSELF. THE OFF-WHITE BUILDING, JUST A SHORT
walk from the center of London, had been surprisingly hard to find, but
there it was. It stood on the corner facing a side street, connected to a
long row of other embassies looking toward the larger Kensington Road.
The black, red, and green flag signaled that I was at the right place.

Having made it apparently right before closing, I searched for an entrance to the building. I had enough trouble locating places as it was—
sadly I am a bit retarded—but in this case it didn't help that it was also
well hidden. It was as if it was conscious of the current ignominy of the
land it represented and, unwilling to face the world boldly, it had con-
cealed itself beneath the work of a construction crew. When I walked in,
I discovered furthermore that the facility itself was actually underground
on the building's bottom floor, as though recessing itself even further in
its attempted self-isolation. But it couldn't hide from me.

"The Embassy of Afghanistan," the sign read. *What a lovely country.*
Surely nothing can go wrong from this point onward, I thought to myself,
giggling a little. I paused to reconsider what I was about to do, but quickly
steeled myself against any line of thought that might keep me from my
current object. I had come with the intention of submitting a request to
visit one of the most dangerous countries on earth and embark on what
I hoped to be the first of many such adventures, and I intended to follow
through. My brief reverie only lasted as long as it took me to realize that

it couldn't possibly be worse than Birmingham, the Detroit of the UK. At least Afghan food was bound to be better than British food, so if I died a miserable death, hopefully it would be on a full and happy stomach. Without a doubt, I am a British supremacist and willing to tell anyone about how much I miss the Empire, but there are some things not even a chauvinist can deny.

Steeling my resolve and stumbling down the stairs, impressed with my own courage, I entered a cramped room that had just enough space to fit the twelve seats arranged there. Not surprisingly, everyone already present was rather swarthier than myself, and all eyes turned to the one White guy who had surely wandered into the wrong room, if not the wrong building. I smiled at them politely before confidently walking across the ornate, traditional carpet and straight up to the COVID glass-covered front desk. Unlike for most countries, E-visas weren't available for Afghanistan—I couldn't imagine why—so if you wanted to go, you had to apply in person at the travel office in the embassy. The lady on the other side of the glass greeted me with a jolly attitude, much the same way you would a lost child.

"Good day, sir! This is the Embassy of Afghanistan. Are you looking for the Dubai Embassy? It's just next door." It sounded like a scenario she had rehearsed well.

"Oh no, I'm in the right place actually." I smiled again with a mischievous twinkle in my eye and proudly laid down my application. "One visa, please." I spoke as though ordering from McDonalds, not visiting the embassy of one of the world's most dangerous nations.

She raised her eyebrows but went along with it. "Yes, sir, and is this a work or a media visa?"

I slid the paper across to her with my finger pointing to a spot on the top of the page with a confident little tap. "A tourism visa, Ma'am."

A look of horror and slight amusement immediately manifested on her face, as well as those of the other staff members in the room who couldn't help but overhear me. Out of the corner of my eye I could see them all look at each other. If facial expressions could speak in sentences, their collective utterance would have been, "This motherfucker is going to die." I was also glad that I hadn't acted on my earlier impulse to jokingly announce "shalom" to the Muslim occupants of this particular room.

Still, she was very kind and, once she got over the initial shock, clearly seemed quite happy with the idea that I wanted to visit her country, regardless of any concerns for my safety. I couldn't help thinking again how ironic this was when I could travel a mere twenty miles south into London and be worried about getting stabbed while I walked down the street. Visiting Afghanistan would be just fine. How much worse than modern London, chock full of football hooligans and Somali migrants, could it be?

The lady hesitated suddenly mid paperwork and turned to inform me of a potential difficulty. Only a day or two earlier, it had been announced that Afghanistan was on the "red" list, meaning that no one should travel due to COVID-19 and if you did, you would have to fork over a couple grand to pay for a hotel to isolate in when you returned to the UK. I thought this was insane and a waste of my time, as COVID wasn't a real concern for someone taking holiday in the Middle East. In any case, I had already found a work-around. Unperturbed, I informed her that my plan was to fly to Albania for ten days on the way back to "self-isolate" and then fly into the UK freely. She caught on, smiling with a wink as if to say "this sneaky bastard," then returned to deciphering my sloppy penmanship.

"Are you going there *just* for tourism?" Her curiosity got the better of her and she clearly couldn't believe that there was no other reason I would venture to her war-torn homeland. I think she must have fancied me to be an aspiring diplomat of some kind, trying to make a name forging peace deals or something. While I did in fact simply want to visit Afghanistan for my own enjoyment, I explained to her further that I would be doing charity work as a Catholic, which was also true. As a Catholic, I try to commit a tenth of my income to charity, and I didn't want it going to some fake humanitarian corporation that would squander it instead of actually helping people. I had put aside the last month of pay from my two part-time jobs, which I kept while also being a full-time student, and wanted to donate that to help people struggling in Afghanistan. The sum came to just under £1,000, which wasn't that much over here but could make a huge difference in that part of the world, I reasoned. Since I had received a generous scholarship to attend university, my two jobs provided me with more of a surplus than any real necessity; certainly the folks in Afghanistan were in a tougher spot than me.

What I wasn't going to tell her was the perception, which I shared with most people in the West, that Afghanistan was a mysterious, far-off land of great curiosity, complete with an alien way of life and lands that no picture could fully explain, just begging to be explored—by me. I had looked at photos and videos while researching the nation for weeks and realized I had to see it with my own eyes. I had a hunch that it wasn't just endless sand and RPGs, even though that would be plenty cool as well. There must be more to this distant place of such ill repute with the leaders of my own country—leaders who I felt so poorly represented me.

Eventually, we exchanged more paperwork, signed some documents, and I was told to wait while she continued her work behind the desk. As she continued opening and closing various filing cabinets and tapping away at her keyboard, I took the opportunity to sit down with the other Afghans in the room, trying to familiarize myself with the sensation of feeling out of place.

Days before, I had hired the cheapest tour guide in the country for about £600 to meet another visa requirement. Although I could have easily fabricated a guide or tour company—something I would do during later travels to other places—since the bureaucrats working at the embassies don't usually verify these things, I had decided against that tactic, as I really wanted this trip to work out. And besides, having at least one face waiting for me when I landed in Kabul would surely be worth what I had paid.

The excitement of sitting silently in a room full of foreign strangers didn't last long. After playing Clash of Clans for twenty minutes, I was called back up and told that I had all the documents required and could leave my passport there; they would mail it back to me with the tourist visa. Traveling to Afghanistan was turning out to be easier than buying a kitchen knife in my own country. I didn't know it at the time, but I learned later that I was the last person ever issued a tourist visa by the US-backed government of Afghanistan.

It's funny to note that the visa required "a personal statement explaining the reason for travel." My response was simply an A4 sheet of paper with only the word "fun" written on it. It was accepted without question. I was ready for my very own White boy summer.

August 12th
Leaving England

THE INTERVENING MONTH SINCE MY VISA APPLICATION PASSED QUICKLY. My visa had processed with no issue and they returned the passport to me as promised. Before I knew it, my departure date was upon me.

Before arriving at London Heathrow Airport, I hardly knew that a place could be so chaotic. I bumped and jostled my way through the double set of glass doors, feeling all around me that contradictory atmosphere of sterility and grime unique to massive hubs of public transportation. I wandered through the maze of corridors and lifts and the pantheon of airlines that promised to bear the teeming, anxious mass of humanity to farther corners of the world than anyone has a right to go. This included me, there on that day on the business of getting myself to probably the world's most extreme vacation destination—Afghanistan.

I arrived four hours before my flight's departure and to ease my own nerves told myself that this was more than enough time to go through security. I suppressed jitters as I prepared myself to be questioned about my trip. I couldn't really blame anyone for being skeptical. "I'm going to Afghanistan for fun" might not cut it with the security and government intelligence.

Arriving at the front desk, I presented my passport and tried not to smile too obnoxiously as I watched the mortified staff member check over my Afghanistan visa as though I had just presented him with Willy Wonka's Golden Ticket. An awkward space of five minutes with fake computer typing passed between us before he settled on an excuse to avoid this headache. He squinted deeply at the visa and then turned to me with a short exhale of self-satisfaction. "This visa isn't valid for another day. Look at the start date; you can only travel from the twelfth of August onwards!"

I'm not sure what was going on with this guy, but I patiently informed him that it was indeed the twelfth of August. His eyes expanded as though he had just time traveled a day into the future. After grumbling and apologizing and making small talk for a few more moments, he gave me more bad news: regulations had been updated a night ago and currently every traveler needed to have a COVID-19 PCR test taken before the flight.

I didn't feel like lying to him about this, and it wouldn't have helped me anyway. Neither, I thought, would trying to explain that COVID and I have a mutual understanding where I won't bother it if it doesn't bother me, which had thus far worked out well. Twinges of disappointment grew in my stomach as I began to worry that my grand adventure might be over before it even started. One of the reasons I had picked glorious Afghanistan as a travel destination in the first place was because the country was open and free from COVID restrictions. I knew that these tests usually take twenty-four hours at minimum, and my flight was departing in only three and a half. The staff offered to move my flight to the next day, but compared to the thrill I had been anticipating of goofing off in Afghanistan that night, the idea felt like an eternity away, and moreover I had no backup plan for a place to stay. I had been homeless for a few months when I was eighteen, but at least on the streets the public benches weren't made out of cold metal with dividers like the ones at the airport.

I considered my options and recalled seeing a poster on a bus on my way to the airport advertising rapid PCR tests. Surely there was a solution to my present crisis. I thanked the still-perturbed staffer for his "help" and rushed out, running through the airport while searching on my phone for nearby clinics. One popped up at a nearby hotel. As I jumped into a taxi flagged down just outside, I could feel my heart in my mouth and the adrenaline pumping in my veins in rhythm with the Doom soundtrack currently playing in my earphones. We came across roadwork blocking the entire street, and I inquired with the driver about the time cost of the diversion. It was far more than I could afford, so I decided I'm better off putting my fate on my own feet. I paid for the trip up to that point and hopped out into the crush of London's pedestrian traffic. I was fully prepared to push aside old ladies and children if I had to—it's the Afghanistan traveler grindset that non-Afghanistan visitors just can't be expected to understand.

The roads and sidewalk ahead were blocked by setting concrete and heavy machinery with warning signs dotted around. Next to all of this, however, was a wall just shy of being taller than me, on the other side of which I needed to be. It had some barbed wire at the top but looked wide enough such that a good section of it could be walked on if someone was retarded enough to do so.

I was retarded enough to do so. I hastily clambered up with my leg brushing against the barbed wire. I then danced my way across the top as though I were on a tightrope at the circus, with concrete and asphalt setting on either side. The workmen, too surprised to react, looked on in amazement. I saw some of the more senior guys shaking their heads as though they endured this kind of stuff every day. A fall into drying concrete would get me in serious trouble with the workers as well as end the chances of a PCR test, but I was on a mission. Nothing and no one would stop me.

I made it to the other side with ease, cutting ten minutes off my trip with the clinic just around the corner. The cost of a few small cuts on my ankle was a small price for precious time. I ran around the back and encountered a large but sparsely occupied parking lot containing the clinic in question, one of those mobile stations that more closely resembled a food truck or moving trailer than a medical testing area. My heart still pounding from the exercise and the urgency of the situation, I gasped out a hurried explanation of why I needed my test to be done in two hours. I brutalized my sinuses with the swab and returned the sample to the attendant while still coughing from the nasal violation. The elderly

Indian lady who checked me in smiled and reassured me that my swab would be moved to the front of the batch. I had no idea if this was true, but it seemed the best I could hope for, so after getting my nose raped, I thanked her profusely and then walked to the corner shop to buy her some chocolate, though honestly, she could have benefited from going on a diet. Maybe it was a bribe, maybe an act of kindness—the reader can make their own judgment—but it did help ensure that I got my PCR test put to the front, as she was surprised and grateful and called me a "kind young man."

After a bit of waiting, I realized that there was no point in standing around the area and nothing really that I could do other than get myself back to the airport. The next two hours were a waiting game during which I unsuccessfully attempted to calm my dancing nerves, pulling down the screen on my phone every few seconds, watching my email in-box, as I walked intently. I nearly ran into several street lamps on my walk back to the airport, so desperate was I not to lose a second as I waited for the test outcome that would determine whether I would wake up the next day on a cold London bench or under the hot Afghan sun. I had no reason to believe the result wouldn't be negative, but still, there was a lot at stake, and you never know with these things.

I popped in at a cafe and pulled out a tactic that I had learned in my homeless days: buy the cheapest drink on the menu and consume it at a pace slower than the rate of evaporation so that I can enjoy a comfortable seat in a cozy area. I leaned back and turned to Netflix to re-watch one of my favorite movies, *American Psycho*. I had to keep pausing this sacred male experience as a 30-something female backpacker occupying a seat at my table kept interrupting with attempts at striking up a conversation despite me politely declining. I realized eventually that it was no use, and I sat in increasing agitation as her endless jabbering clashed most disconcertingly with the ticking clock in my head counting down to my flight's departure and reminding me that I still didn't have that test. After hearing about her life story for almost an hour, I was nearly bored to tears and was becoming certain I'd miss the plane. Momentary relief came as I spotted a free space at a fast-food restaurant and politely excused myself, wishing her a pleasant holiday to the exotic and far-away destination of Spain where she was going to "find herself."

At the fast-food restaurant, I was informed that I had to order something to sit down despite the place being empty, so I obliged by choosing the cheapest burger available and customizing it to be overly complex to make. When it arrived, I didn't take a bite and instead sat back to listen to the gentleman next to me bragging about his life over the phone to try to impress someone he was clearly flirting with. I noticed the ring on his finger and assumed the best, thinking that he probably got a promotion or something and was calling home to inform his better half, until the actual strain of the conversation interrupted to rudely shatter my mental generosity. "She won't find out, babe; you know I love you instead; things have been over with her for years" was the most egregious line I heard. If your name is Margaret and you have a husband who's five-foot-ten with brown hair and tanned white skin who was in Heathrow on August 12th, please use this book and my testimony in your divorce case. If there's one type of person I dislike immensely, it's a cheater.

This reminded me of a similar situation on a previous holiday when I was with a friend in Norway. There had been an obnoxious businessman bragging about his life loudly on the phone just like that guy, almost as if he was shouting it to the crowd for approval from strangers who, not knowing him, might actually believe he was important enough to justify being so publicly annoying. As it turned out, he was likely just compensating for insecurity about his status. My friend and I had the idea to gaslight him by doing the same thing behind him, trying to one-up what we heard with wild stories about getting paid a 200k bonus and complaining about how it was far beneath our expectations, repeating things that he would say and incorporating them into our own conversation to shut down his ego. We burst out laughing when the clerk at the front desk informed him that his card had been declined.

After a bit of daydreaming prompted by these reflections, I stole a glance at the tiny little time stamp in the top corner of my phone. There were only ten minutes remaining before boarding started and I still had not received the test result needed to get past the check-in desk and security. My heart sank, and I had almost lost hope and was in the midst of asking for Divine help when finally, with two minutes left, I got a notification from the testing center. I frantically unlocked my phone, scrambled to my email, in my haste scrolling past the link to view the results, and finally saw the word "NEGATIVE."

Jamming my phone in my pocket and knocking over the chair I was sitting in, I grabbed my bag and jumped the little seating area fence, throwing my untouched "food" in the bin. The fast food was likely a greater danger to my health than any place I might be heading to—at least in Afghanistan everything didn't have soy in it. I was to learn later that during their occupation, the US government had implemented a program costing millions of dollars to try to introduce soybeans to the Afghan diet. Like the fate of so many military campaigns in the region, the valiant efforts of the Americans were not successful. The wise Afghan people simply didn't like the taste.

I had just ten minutes of boarding time to get to the gate of the plane before it took off without me. I returned to the check-in desk of my airline with a wide smile, enjoying the pure mortification on the face of the same man who thought he'd gotten rid of me. I informed him that I had gotten the test done in time. Once he rushed me through, I immediately ran to the airport security, which by some stroke of luck was nearly empty.

I had my bag searched and was informed by a female officer that my aftershave container was over 100 ml. I was not allowed to take it even though it was ninety percent empty. Stupid, but of course I didn't want to cause issues for the staff—they were just doing their job after all and don't make the rules—so I removed the cap in front of her and drenched myself in the remaining contents. I now smelled amazing if a little flammable. She laughed at the antic and struck up a conversation asking about my destination. I was wary of setting off alarm bells by stating that I'm on my way to the fun, family vacation hotspot of Afghanistan, but to my surprise she didn't bat an eye and let me continue through, wishing me a pleasant holiday.

"Stay safe," she joked.

"Thanks. If you see me on the news, it's gone bad," I replied with a smile, unaware at the time of the irony. Looking back, I hope she remembers that conversation.

After setting off on a run once again, I arrived in time to board the plane with less than three minutes before the gate closed. I could hear the *Mission Impossible* theme playing in my head as I sat down and thanked God for answering my prayer.

I settled into my narrow economy seat with cracked vinyl upholstery. Nothing had felt so satisfying all day. Absentmindedly I took a second look at the PCR test email and noticed that it was really just a standard letter in the form of a PDF, with no QR code to scan or any other unique way to verify that it was genuine. I amused myself, considering how I could have cheated the system and created the same document within five minutes to save me the trouble.

Got on the flight, literally gates and 2 mins afterwards I was allowed to board. I ran to boarding and got in on time. Praise God!

Holding my ticket to Kabul

Just before takeoff, one of the stewardesses, a young Afghan woman in a black hijab, came by to ask me to put my AirPods away so that I could listen to the safety demonstration. I asked if I could use mufflers so that my ears didn't pop, and she said yes, so when she turned away, I just put my headphones over my AirPods and continued listening to music because I don't respect European Union Aviation Safety Agency rules, or for that matter the EU in general. The lady informed me that I can't have headphones on, but I told her they're acting as ear mufflers and showed her that the cable wasn't plugged in to prove that they're off, so she apologized and moved on. I've never understood the no electronics during takeoff rule and never made much attempt to do so as I had no intentions of following it.

The plane climbed, and soon we reached cruising altitude, and I could see the staff starting to make their way through the cabin passing out meals. I'd never had airline food beyond a packet of crisps, and I was excited and prepared to find out if the rumors were true. I asked myself if the common joke "what's the deal with airline food?" actually had a pun at the end or if it's just lost to time. When the cart rolled around to me, I was delighted and beyond grateful to realize it's free. A further wave of relief washed over me when I then looked through the ingredients and saw no soy or artificial chemicals. I wolfed it down and came to the conclusion that it's actually better than almost all food in England, which, as mentioned, isn't really a high standard. The lady sitting adjacent to me offered me hers as well, saying she wasn't hungry, and I gratefully accepted and scarfed it down. As the attendants were collecting my leftover trays, I asked how much it would cost to buy an additional meal, thinking about the journey back as I was expecting to be on the same Turkish airline. However, there must have been a language barrier, as instead of answering the lady just handed me another meal for free, which I didn't object to.

After a layover in Istanbul, the next stop was Afghanistan. Originally my flight plan had included more stops because that was, somehow, the cheapest route available according to the comparison website I used. A few weeks before departure, however, one of the flights got canceled, messing up the entire trip. I was refused a refund and instead offered fifty percent back in company credit. This was a galling suggestion, but it's not like the flight company actually had a say in the matter because I simply did a chargeback and got everything back, claiming on the canceled flight insurance and making a profit. After that I was able to find a more straightforward route that was now cheaper than the original tickets.

I had a few hours before my final flight and I wanted to explore, so I started wandering around the Istanbul airport. While in the duty-free section, a gentleman approached and informed me that he offered cheap insurance for my holiday. Obviously, I wasn't interested in his product, but I felt like wasting some time, so after some small talk and enduring his sleazy salesman pitch, I informed him of my destination. It took him a few minutes to process that I was using the words "Afghanistan" and "tourism" together without sarcasm, but after that he opened up and seemed to put the sales pitch aside and become his normal self as he got quite engrossed in hearing about my plans. I told him that I was going there to do some charity work in the form of handing out a months' pay in cash to people I came across who needed it. He leaned in with the most serious expression and asked if I'm part of the CIA and this was some sort of training mission. I had to try not to laugh to keep from offending him. I could tell he just couldn't accept that I was really going there for tourism, so I decided to play along, looking to either side to check my surroundings before answering with a grave face. "We don't send our people here on their first day," I replied with a wink. I shook his hand firmly with a smile and left him looking stunned as I walked away.

I decided to sit down near the terminal in one of those circular seats that fit six or so people. After a few minutes a small Asian lady hobbled up to me, head leaned over and hands wobbling on her cane, and asked if she could have my seat so she and her granddaughter could sit together. Of course I obliged, jumping up and helping her slowly recline herself into my spot, for which she thanked me kindly. The little girl sat next to her. I wandered away a bit to wait for a new seat to open up. After about half an hour I looked up from my phone as she was getting up and almost glanced away, but my gaze was arrested by the sight of her shooting to her feet, picking up the little girl with one arm, putting the cane under the other, and walking away with perfect posture. I would like to think she was either extremely tired before and regained her strength by sitting down or maybe shot up some steroids while I wasn't looking, but neither explanation is likely, so I have to accept I was probably just conned. I had to respect the brilliance of the act though, and I wasn't about to give her game away. I just hoped that I could be like her one day when I'm an old man.

The terminal display flashed that my flight to Kabul was ready for boarding. I didn't want another scare like at Heathrow, so I got on the move. At the boarding area, the lady just glanced at my PCR test without a care and let me in to join the sixty or so people already waiting there. I noticed a well-built White man who looked like a modern version of Rambo standing by the entrance to the jet bridge playing with compartments inside the wall. He looked like an interesting target for conversation, so I walked up to him and introduced myself.

"What's taking you to Afghanistan?" I asked as I shook his beefy hand.

He responded in a friendly tone, "I run an infrastructure construction company."

"So you're the man who builds the roads?"

"Roads, bridges, highways, you name it. Build new ones, repair old ones."

"Is it a thriving market in Afghanistan?"

He laughed. "No, not at all, which is why I get paid stupid amounts, because no one else wants to be there doing it."

"So true. Are you paid by the Afghan government? The Americans?"

"Western governments generally, yes," he answered before turning my attention to the wall compartment he was fidgeting with that contained wires and a switch. "What do you suppose all this does?" he asked with a mischievous smile.

"Is it a breaker panel? You'd think it would be more secure if it's something important. Has no one yelled at you yet?"

"Nope! What do you say, should we turn the lights off for a second?"

This man was goofing off harder than me, I realized. He laughed again and removed his finger from the switch. "Not today, eh?"

A third White guy walked up to join us, clearly glad to find fellow Europeans to make conversation with. He was more bookish and not as tall and looked about forty, though with the far-off stare of a sixty-year-old war vet. He told us that he worked at the embassy in Kabul, which reassured me because it seemed to mean that the embassy staff were not leaving Afghanistan at that time. He clearly didn't love his job as much as my first friend, though, and told us how he doesn't get enough even with hazard pay. He then asked me what I'm going to Afghanistan for. I didn't mention the charity work, as it was too meager to brag about, so I told him I'm just popping down for holiday. Unfortunately, he didn't seem to appreciate the light-heartedness. His already tired visage seemed to age even more, his face dropping and eyes glazing over, as though he'd just let go of a fake smile he'd been wearing for the last few years. Without hesitation, he just told me that he may see me in the embassy in the next few weeks and walked away.

As more people boarded the flight, I realized the plane was quickly filling and would be packed to the brim. I was lucky to have a seat next to a window. The takeoff was uneventful apart from my brief realization that this was my last opportunity to turn back, a thought I tossed aside as soon as it formed. An Afghan lad in his early twenties had sat down next to me, with others who appeared to be his friends taking seats near us. The young man looked worried and tense when he saw me. I shared a snack I had brought in my backpack and he lightened up, trying out the few broken English words he knew in attempting to converse with me. He seemed to want to watch a nature documentary but hadn't been provided with wired headphones for the built-in TV on the back of the airplane seats. He was too socially awkward to ask for a set, or possibly just unaware that they were free. I flagged down a flight attendant, and she kindly brought some over for him. I was now cool with the Afghan lads. They became enamored with my skeleton watch and asked if they could see it, so I handed it over and let them pass it around and shine it

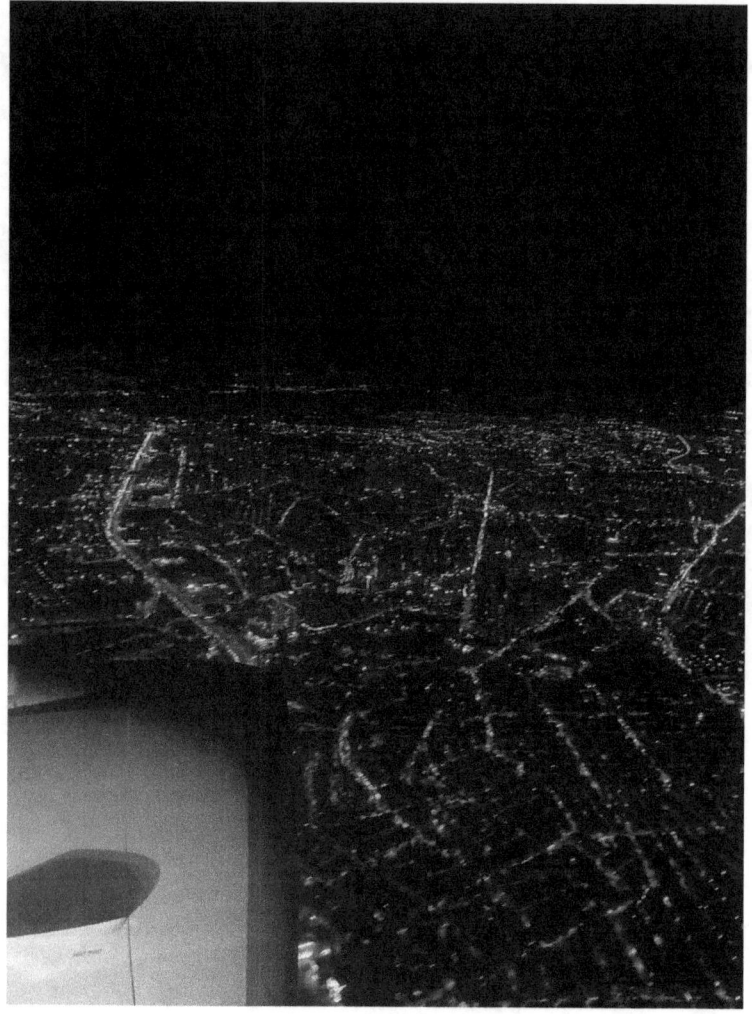

View of Istanbul after takeoff

in the light. Little did they know it only cost me 15 quid off Ebay. It did look cool though, and eventually they gave it back. Later while I was watching the same nature documentary, the lad next to me pointed to a polar bear eating a seal and exclaimed, "I AM BIG FISH I AM POWER." I nodded in agreement, appreciating the sentiment.

It being the same Turkish airline, the same dishes were served as on the other flight, which somewhat surprised me as I was still unused to the luxury of free food while flying. I picked the kebab. Despite all the jokes, I found airline food amazing. After eating my fourth dinner that day, I passed my American Express card to the flight attendant and asked politely if I could buy another two dishes for the journey. She examined it and, noticing the title, looked back at me impressed. "Lord?"

"Lord Miles," I answered, smiling widely. She beamed, her voice suddenly increasing in pitch as her attitude became noticeably more bubbly.

"No charge, Lord Miles. I'll go and get that for you." As I ate my fifth free kebab dinner and stowed away the sixth for later, I reflected on the lordship certificate being one of the best lifehacks I'd done in a while. For those who haven't clued in to this yet, I legally have the title of "lord" but not through inheritance. I once came across an advert on social media for a gag gift lord certificate, purchased it, and realized that it looked stupidly premium. The idea came to me to confidently stroll into a bank wearing a suit and putting on my best posh accent to ask to change my name to include the title of "lord" as I'd recently been bestowed it. I timed this around peak business hours when the bank employees were too busy to care and was able to get them to put "Lord Miles Routledge" on my account, including my credit file and every card I owned. Since then, whenever I book anything I regularly get free upgrades on flights and hotels because they think I'm actually important.

I decided to wait and not use the tiny airplane bathroom, as I didn't want to drop a bomb on Afghanistan. After the nature documentary was finished, I turned on BBC News. There was a grainy live broadcast playing about the current situation in Afghanistan. The TV showed the Taliban had moved further up towards Kabul with little resistance. I pointed this out to my newfound group of Afghan friends with worry on my face, to which they responded by cheering and celebrating, with indeed most of the cabin erupting into joy at the sight of the same broadcast. I didn't want to get on the wrong side of them, so I smiled and cheered along. This marked perhaps the first time in my life that I cheered for a revolutionary terrorist organization, but it was 3:00 a.m. and I was too tired to become a head on a stick. For the last couple hours of the flight, I caught some precious sleep to close the long day.

August 13th
Arriving in Afghanistan

I AWOKE AROUND 6:00 A.M. TO THE AFGHAN SUNRISE WARMING MY FACE. Looking through my window, I saw only an ocean of sandy deserts as far as the eye beheld, pockmarked with tiny villages in the middle of nowhere. In some areas, I could see no possible road or path to reach them, and most looked like they had been made of clay five hundred years ago, remaining unaltered since by the passage of time or the demands of the outside world. I felt transported suddenly to a very different place and time than the one I had left less than twenty-four hours ago. The sunrise cast a shadow for each hill of sand, which gave away their true height, towering over the little villages and other evidence of miniscule humanity. It was a beautiful sight, and I sat in disbelief for a good five minutes watching the sea of sand pass by. I asked myself if I would be able to cross such deserts if worse came to worst and wondered about those hardy people who lived their whole lives there. I could see water in many places from the air, but would I be able to find it if I was on the ground? How would I pass those mountains? Feeling humbled, I realized why so many empires had failed to conquer this country.

Looking around me, I saw that most of the plane remained asleep. An overwhelming smell of sweat and leather sandals hung in the air. I focused for the first time on the smell of normal Afghan males around me. It was an odor akin to that of the average atheist Reddit user, but then again this wasn't a surprise. I could have predicted as much with how greasy their faces were. So much oil, no wonder the Americans invaded!

As people started to awaken, the announcement came that we would be landing in five minutes and were all asked to fasten our seatbelts. The turbulence increased, probably because the pilot was not very good. As we descended, I put my AirPods in again and listened to the song "Freebird." Through the window, I began to see large swaths of greenery with areas of yellow and brown sand. The airport came into sight, and I saw there were farms and makeshift houses right alongside it. I quickly pulled out my phone and took a snapchat video of the landing, uploading it with the caption "It begins Oioi," right as the plane hit the ground, jostling us around as its wheels connected with the runway.

I had made it to Afghanistan.

As we were landing, I noticed that part of the area immediately surrounding the airport was taken up by what looked like a farm right outside the fence that surrounded the runway. There were fields of crops

View of Afghanistan before landing

Another view of Afghanistan

and people leading herds of dusty goats. I could make out several obviously elderly people walking around the area. One man with a plaid turban just stood staring at the plane. It was crazy to think about them living out an ancient, primitive lifestyle right next to a modern marvel of aviation. I wondered what other changes their collective eyes had seen and why they had remained the way they were. Perhaps they were Ted Kaczynski fans and had chosen to reject industrial society. Or perhaps the various regimes propped up as proxies of one empire or another were too dysfunctional to sustain the necessary infrastructure. Regardless, they had no drip with those sun-bleached sandy robes—at least this was my first impression.

The landing was not elegant, though the runway was smooth. The plane shook and rumbled like an old boat tearing at the seams on stormy waves. I watched as some of the young Afghan fliers stood up, thinking that the plane had already landed, and had their inexperience rewarded by being knocked over and falling face first. The Turkish staff looked mortified but also tired, as though they couldn't help smirking at the smarting young lads but knew from experience that there was nothing they could have said to dissuade them and had just been hoping this flight would be different. That lesson didn't stop the tomfoolery, however, and the Afghan boys who had remained seated started laughing and slapping the heads of those who fell down, with their fathers slapping them as well in punishment and yelling disapproval in their unintelligible language. They were all goofing off and having fun. I smiled; it was a raucous good time.

Everyone piled out of the aircraft. As I stepped through the door, I was assaulted with the sensation of the new place I had arrived in. A wave of heat hit me like nothing I'd experienced before. The best comparison I can make is to think of that burning feeling in your eyes when you open the oven too close to your face and how the intense heat can make you feel tired. There is a theory that some regions of the world developed slower than the rest—consider Africa's tallest structures being anthills before the discovery of those lands by people who had built castles and cathedrals—because the hot air made them tired and complacent with their surroundings. After seeing and feeling what I did there in Afghanistan, I could honestly believe it.

The Kabul airport was bizarre. I was glad to see that there were no shops with overpriced knickknacks crowding the space, but what did greet me inside was a small room, no bigger than a master bedroom, with seventies-style dark wood paneling on the walls and floors that depressed the atmosphere and made it feel dim and musty. I was the only White person in the room, a sensation I was familiar with as I could experience much the same in many regions of London, and honestly probably with less personal risk. It didn't faze me in the slightest; I was far too excited with absorbing every detail of my surroundings and soaking in as much as I could manage of this fantastic new land.

The two White guys from before must've had some clearance and therefore managed to escape customs and didn't end up in the same place. I was either of no curiosity to the people waiting in line or they were simply too busy and ignored me; after all, it had been decades since the invasion, so they were surely used to seeing Westerners here in the capital.

I handed over my passport to the border guard sitting in a small wooden booth. He looked absolutely miserable, which is a British national pastime, so I could sympathize. He stared at my tourist visa for a solid minute, his eyes glazing over, and I could all but hear his thoughts about having encountered the biggest retard currently in Asia. After politely swallowing his comments, he dryly asked me to scan my fingers on the machine. This was an alien concept to me, but it turned out that almost every resident, and apparently visitor, in Afghanistan had all of their fingers, thumbs, and palms in a database. I learned later from my tour guide that this was called the Afghan Automatic Biometric Identification System, or AABIS, which the US had implemented to prevent terrorists from flying in and out. I looked at my phone just to double check that it was indeed 2021 and not 1984, before I too decided to keep my comments to myself. There was no going back now. I reasoned to myself that, if necessary, in the future I can just shave or burn my fingerprints off when I get bored or decide to commit tax fraud.

My visa was stamped and the gates swung open like the doors to a Wild West saloon. There was Afghanistan before my eyes, with brilliant and clear blue skies and air so hot it felt like it was boiling despite being so dry. The sun seemed somehow brighter than I had remembered it, which was probably an accurate impression given my native land's propensity for concealing it behind thick malingering clouds. Upon exiting the door, I noticed three people standing there waiting, watching people come out, and I knew what was about to happen. I heard them speaking in their nonsensical native language, and sure enough after a few seconds one approached me with the most comically evil, villain smile on his face possible. He asked in broken English if I knew where the exit was. I decided to play along and said no, acting like a confused tourist. Please note for context that I was currently on a one-way path in the airport, so it's not like there was an excess of options.

He grinned with crooked, gapped teeth like a cartoonish predator that had just lured an unsuspecting prey into a trap and said that he would show me. After walking with me around the corner for literally five seconds, he stopped closer to me and said proudly, "Now you pay!"

I smiled. I had just landed in Afghanistan, and here I was already being cornered against a dusty wall by a greasy, Aladdin villain. I didn't feel scared or even concerned at all; it tickled me that he thought he could intimidate and scam me into giving him money he hadn't earned, and with so little effort. If he had gone out of his way to make the scam more elaborate, I might at least have respected the hustle. Such a lazy scam would have left him starving on the street in a week in London.

I had of course come here with charitable funds looking to give money away to those who needed it, but this man certainly did not seem like the right sort. I also noticed an iphone in his hand that was 2 generations newer than mine. If anything, I should have been asking *him* for a tenner!

I repeated his words. "Now I pay?"

"Now you pay."

"*Now I pay?*" I kept repeating his words back at him, more sarcastic and louder each time, without breaking eye contact. He got more and more nervous, but kept answering "yes" each time. After four or five repeats, it appeared that a sense of guilt was not forthcoming and I had had enough with the game. I pulled out my wallet to his surprise and started flicking through the $100 notes—I had brought most of the money in US dollars, which I assumed would be more useful. I saw his eyes widen and the edges of his mouth creep up again as he dared to hope he would be so lucky. After making a show of displaying the contents of my wallet, I finally pulled out a single pound coin and slapped it into his hand and gave him a cheeky wink.

He acted angry, and I was amazed at the greed of this man, who sported a new generation iPhone and yet felt so entitled to receive hundreds of dollars for his sad little grift. I reasoned that if we were going by the average Afghan salary and were to calculate the hourly rate, he was getting vastly overpaid. I wished him a good day and told him to act like a better Muslim next time. To my surprise, he nodded as if taking the advice and walked away, surely to wait for his next victim. I would meet many honorable people during my time in Afghanistan, but he was not one.

As I walked further, I glanced to the side and saw a brawny White dude with a thick, black beard loading some supplies into an armored vehicle with a few others. I watched them until they drove away, in what I gathered to be the general direction of the exit, and headed there. I found twelve-foot-high metal gates behind which hundreds of Afghans were crowded, pressing against them, waving signs or jumping in the air, while guards from the Afghan National Army (ANA) patrolled up and down the area.

I spotted my tour guide sporting some cool-looking sunglasses. I myself was wearing a pair of stylish aviators, and when he saw me he grinned wide and immediately recognized a brother. His name was Mohammed, but he usually went by Alem. We greeted each other with a firm handshake, and he helped me load my luggage into his van. Alem also introduced me to his brother, who was there with him and who would serve as our driver for the entirety of the trip. I popped my head in and saw a full-sized living room carpet on the floor and stickers covering up the

Solar panels at Kabul airport

lower forty percent of the windshield. I felt amazed that he was able to even drive the contraption, but he was. I had to respect his skill and his style.

At this moment, I remembered a cool fact about Afghanistan from previous research. In a lot of Muslim countries, since alcohol was and always had been illegal, no one ever bothered to invent laws against drunk driving, so there technically weren't any, which I found pretty funny. In fact, there were frequently few traffic laws at all and often no requirement for a driver's license. It would have been perfectly legal for me to drive drunk in a car without any insurance or driving experience. In reality this apparently rarely happened, as most young Afghan men were taught how to drive by their fathers by the age of sixteen. Their fathers would then let them drive so that they themselves could sleep in the back on long, cross-country journeys. The Afghan roads were a wild free-for-all of cacophonous swerving, squealing, and honking. It was chaos compared to my experience in Europe, but the drivers were incredibly skilled at safely navigating the chaos they created.

I thought to myself that if I ever decided to drink alcohol, I'd want to booze cruise down the Afghan highway blasting eighties rock in an American muscle car.

I clambered into the discolored front passenger seat and we set off through the streets of Kabul. Alem began telling me about how the roads weren't busy that day because it was Friday, which is the Islamic religious day of rest called Al-Jumah during which everyone halts their trade and businesses to remember Allah. It was their equivalent of the Christian Sunday, with the exception that they appeared to practice out of genuine religious fervor, as opposed to the majority of Westerners who are often Godless heathens just benefitting materially from Christian holidays. As a comparative Catholic zealot next to many of my secular countrymen, I respected these devout people's fervent opposition to the cynical cancer that is atheism.

Upon leaving the airport grounds, a group of ten or so children, both boys and girls all no older than nine or ten, ran directly up in front of our car, which was going a fair 30 mph. I jolted forward in my seat, bracing against the dashboard as Alem's brother slammed on the brakes. They milled around excitedly much closer than I thought was safe for them, clearly begging for money. I began to reach into my pocket to dispense some charity, but Alem saw me and chuckled.

"They are not poor. Their parents are middle class and live right here in nice houses. They use their cute children for easy money from foreigners who assume every Afghan child is poor."

I stopped my hand, but apparently at least one of the children had understood him too, because his face suddenly changed to a scowl and he held up a middle finger. Shouting to each other in a little chorus like a murder of crows, they ran away down a different road.

After an hour of twisting and turning down the dusty roads of Kabul, we arrived at the city center, where apparently even on Fridays the traffic congestion was quite bad. Beaten up, old Toyota compacts honked and jolted just inches from each other in total gridlock as far as my eyes could see.

Kabul was much flatter than the typical downtown of a Western city. The center area was laid out in a grid, though that apparently rarely helped the traffic situation. Most buildings that I saw were no taller than two or three stories. Some of them were clearly trying to emulate Western styles, which resulted in an alien feeling. Some buildings that we passed were downright tiny and even had corrugated metal or straw roofs. There were small markets or individual shops where it looked like people were doing metalwork, selling carpets, and conducting other business. While many shops were closed due to the holy day, some were open. Alem told me that these people were very poor and basically had no choice but to keep working, so the authorities let it slide. Barbed wire was very common to see crowning the walls of even small stores or houses.

On one of the taller buildings we passed, I saw digital billboards advertising Samsung phones, which gave me a pang of disappointment that even here, in a desert city in one of the most dangerous countries in the world, I was still within the reach of globalized tech consumerism. I was glad, however, to see that the sides of the streets were not choked up with flashing, LED-emblazoned storefronts of fast-food chains and vape shops—indeed, I saw none of the latter at all—as they have increasingly become in every European city. Almost every store I saw seemed one-of-a-kind and independent, with little to no corporate branding. At most, there was the occasional aesthetic, sun-bleached poster with nineties stock imagery.

Driving downtown

Traffic in Kabul

A layer of sand and dust permanently settled on all the streets, keeping the air dry and occasionally getting kicked up in clouds by people or vehicles. Between the street and the sidewalk, there were open drains sometimes as deep as three feet, clogged with trash and refuse that attracted swarms of flies. The atmosphere of garbage and grime from this was enhanced by the rivers that flowed through Kabul, which were also full of trash and had a greenish color that didn't bode well for the potability of their domestic water. That said, however, the roads themselves seemed to be in excellent condition, as had the modern tarmac at the airport, all of which made me question whether my taxes had been going to fix a rather different set of potholes than the ones that plagued transportation on the streets back home. Alem later confirmed that most of the paved asphalt roads in central Kabul had been funded directly by the US government. I wouldn't be surprised if the UK also contributed. On the outskirts of the city, where roads were poorer, if potholes did appear, the locals would often fill them in with sand, dirt, or rubble and then charge a tax to those who drove over their work. Apparently, this was so normalized that it essentially ran on the honor system, and most people would pay without being asked. If they had the money to afford a decent car, they could afford the road tax. Chuffed, I smiled to myself when I heard this. I had no idea that Afghanistan was such a libertarian dream.

Kabul was truly a sight to behold.

One of the polluted rivers in Kabul

We pulled up to the place I would be staying for the night, and I got out to take a look around. On the opposite side of the street I saw an iron gated park with many families lounging on the grass or under the trees in the shade. Children ran around chasing each other screaming with delight and getting into mischief while street vendors sold freshly made food and second-hand clothes. I thought about one of the biggest trage-dies in the West, the over-regulation of food by government bodies. Sure the street food I saw may have caused me to destroy the toilet for two days afterward, but at least it would be tasty and cheap and without nasty soy or endocrine disrupting seed oils.

I looked around on my side of the street, searching for some indication of a hotel or inn, but was perplexed that there seemed to be none. I stood in front of a large metal wall with several coils of barbed wire running along the top, as I'd seen on many other structures. Its surface was filled up entirely with all kinds of posters. Afghan men, presumably politicians, smiled at me from behind ethnically typical, long, slightly thin beards. Beneath the newest layer of posters were still more, older posters. On either side of this wall were two brick walls, each overgrown with greenery and vines. I couldn't see a door or even a window anywhere.

Alem called my attention to the metal wall right in front of me, and as he approached it, I noticed a small slit in the middle at about eye height. He was carrying a document that confirmed our hotel booking and slipped it in, shouting something that he later translated for me: "Do not be lazy brother, let us in!"

Suddenly the wall began to move, and I realized that the section we were standing in front of was not part of the wall at all, but a twelve-foot-tall metal barricade that was so camouflaged in posters that anyone who didn't look very closely would assume it was just a continuation of the brick on either side. After we walked through that, we found ourselves in a small area in front of another door where we got patted down and searched. At that point I noticed the CCTV cameras mounted on the wall along with the barbed wire, monitoring each side. The wall was thick and moved with a slow momentum that belied its immense weight. I felt like I was entering a tiny fortress. It was an impressive compound.

After we passed the search, we were allowed through the actual door. I stepped through, glad to get out of the dust and heat of the Kabul streets, and suddenly found myself inside a pleasant garden area that took me by surprise. Roses covered the walls, and trees lent generous overhanging branches to provide shade. A row of exotic flowers hugged the path with grass of a brilliant emerald green dotted around. To the left was a large birdhouse and to the right a table with a chessboard and two matching chairs set neatly around it.

I paused for a moment, mouth agape at this lovely little patch of greenery thriving in the middle of a dusty country, tucked away behind brick walls and barbed wire surrounded by so much litter and chaos. Quite frankly the space was rather nicer than anything I could remember from my hometown.

The garden at the hotel

As I approached the actual entrance to the hotel building, two gentlemen came out and grabbed my bags, which gave me flashbacks to my mugging in Birmingham. I managed to suppress this as they looked at me with deferential, almost servile eagerness, and it was apparent that they only wanted to take them to my room for me, a touch of luxury not even my Lordly title had afforded me historically. All I needed to do was leave the country and go to a part of the former Empire to really be treated like a noble. Alem showed me the main lobby, which contained a vending machine for water, and the dining hall for breakfast. He was telling me more about the place when one of the owners came over to chat us up. I was told that not many people stay here. It was a family-run business, and normally their primary traffic was visitors from Pakistan, with a Westerner only every few months. However, recently the numbers had dropped dramatically, for which they seemed quite resentful of the West, claiming that our media had been sensationalizing everything going on in Afghanistan, making the country out to be a deadly and unstable place on the verge of collapse. The man went on quite a rant about this, and about how the Taliban will never take over Kabul. I agreed because I'd heard the same thing from my tour guide, the airline staff, my Afghan friends in England, the embassy, and the media.

I was presented with a takeout menu. "If you want lunch, sir, there is a restaurant a few miles away. They do delivery. Good local food. I must warn you though, it is pricey."

I took the menu, curious as to what the man considered to be a "pricey" meal. "Thank you. How expensive is it? What's the typical price?"

"I'm afraid it's a minimum of $2 spending and $1 delivery fee."

I tried not to smile and decided to play along. "That is expensive, but I think I may be able to pull together the funds." The man had no way of knowing that I had almost a thousand pounds on me. The information about the price put things in perspective for me, and I realized that I should have no problems funding the rest of the trip. That, or maybe he was messing with me and that was actually an affordable price for most people who stayed at the hotel.

A picture of the menu

At this point I wanted to check out my room, so I went up the stairs to the second floor. Upon entering, I was delighted to find a large double bed, a phat CRT TV alongside a desk, a personal shower, and a functioning AC unit mounted on the wall. It was double the size of my old student accommodation in England, and with more amenities. I did a quick calculation in my head of the monthly cost of rent here in contrast to back home. At around half the price, it really made me start to consider relocating to Afghanistan permanently. My tour guide helped me connect to the Wi-Fi, which I got at speeds of 30 Mbps, a whole ten times faster than what I was used to. Despite my accommodation in England being literally the cheapest one within a ten-mile radius of my home town, I still began to feel like I was really being ripped off the more that I compared it to where I was now. Afghanistan was turning out to be a hidden gem. I asked Alem if this was a normal hotel, and he stated that the "normal" hotels listed on Google often got targeted by ISIS-K suicide bombers— the Afghanistan-specific ISIS branch, referring to the Khorasan region they were based in—or Taliban soldiers. This hotel was kept secret, even from locals living nearby.

My hotel room

While settling in, I talked some more with Alem. He was fantastically knowledgeable and an excellent guide throughout the whole trip. He is a very good man, but sadly we would later have a falling out when he dropped his support of a second trip I'd planned to help him get out of the country, into which I invested a lot of time planning and money that was generously donated by others. Regardless, during my first visit to Afghanistan, he put a tremendous amount of effort into organizing things for me, like this hotel, or taking me to places I would find interesting, all of which I am immensely grateful for.

He told me tales of his time working for the US military, which he'd done for over ten years to provide for his family. He had a degree in pharmacy but had found that working for the occupiers or as a tour guide for foreigners in general was a thousand times more profitable. Apparently, young Afghans had the same issue as many people in the West who go to university, in that everyone had a degree and the job market was saturated. In fact, everyone in Kabul was entitled to free university tuition if they had met an easily obtainable standard during their studies. Moreover, even the top-paying and most prestigious jobs in the West like doctors, lawyers, teachers—the standard educated commercial jobs—paid less than $100 or $200 a month. Politicians perhaps made more, but other than that, the only way to really make a good living and climb was international business. In comparison with these prospects, people who could translate or serve as guides for the US military would be paid up to $70 a day, which in that context was insanely good.

Before we went out, Alem handed me some traditional Afghan clothes to try on. The typical male Afghan fit is called a *perahan tunban*. It's a two-piece set, with a top that's similar to a long-sleeved shirt and long pants for the bottom. Both parts are wavy and loose-fitting, giving you plenty of breathing room. The top *perahan* part is like a shirt but extends down as far as the knees. Sometimes it would have a collar, and I saw lots of men who wore a vest over it. Alem gave me a set that was a light purple, which he told me was because I was a lord and therefore deserved a royal color.

I put on the clothing and took a look in the mirror set up near the door in my room. The *tunban*, the trousers, were tied using string like loose pajamas would be, and the top was soft and free-fitting like a thin jumper. Paired with the heat it was insanely comfortable, and I could no longer scoff at the old goat-herders I'd seen earlier outside the airport. My initial impression that these people were too poor or backward to have proper fitting clothing was replaced by respect for the effectiveness of their garb. I could now see why this was the drip of choice. Accusations of cultural appropriation never bothered me much, but even if they had, I would have half a mind to adopt the fashion even upon my return home.

Putting on Afghan clothes

Still wearing my cross

We hit the town, and on the way, I gave out some of the money I'd brought for charity. There was a woman begging on a street corner, and we stopped to talk with her for a few minutes and learned she and her family had fallen on hard times. I gave her about $100, which she was immensely grateful for. It was probably more money than she'd ever seen in her life, and I was very glad I could make a difference in the life of that family. I also gave money to some children who Alem confirmed were more genuine than the previous bunch we had come across by the airport.

There was a lot of poverty in Afghanistan, and I was under no illusions that I could address it all or really make any impact on a systemic level, but I hoped God would make use of the small charity I could provide. I had been homeless myself not too long ago, and I felt incredibly blessed by my lot in life now. In the first couple days of the trip, I gave away all the money I brought, mostly to beggars, as well as refugees from the Taliban and other people who were particularly poor.

Alem suggested that we check out Kabul's infamous bird market. I was a bit confused initially, although willing to go—a bird market in Afghanistan sounded like an interesting experience regardless—but as we went along, he explained more of the context of the place. Many of the birds were not sold to eat, but to keep as pets or to fight. As I strolled along by his side, enjoying the comfortable swish of my new, well-ventilated getup and the curious but friendly glances of the locals, I observed not just hens and roosters, but pigeons, quail, finches, canaries, parrots, partridge, and more. I was surprised by the variety.

"Are these all from Afghanistan?" I asked him.

"No, no! From Afghanistan, from Pakistan, from Iran, from other places. People don't just catch the birds, they buy them, bring them here to fight, to sell. Lots of birds from all over the world."

I was becoming used to the streets of Afghanistan and the accompanying smell of battery acid, smog, and sewage, but the olfactory concussion of the bird market was another shock entirely. The smell of feces and birdseed was thick in the air, but I could almost ignore it as I focused on the strange beauty of this place. Grimy as it was, there was vital charm to it. As I turned to get a look at the entire scene, I was transported back in time several hundred years, surrounded by middle-aged and elderly men in robes and turbans inspecting birds, peeking through cages, bartering, showing off, and arguing. Not a silicone chip or LED touch screen in sight, just people living in the moment. I smirked to myself at the near unconscious, post ironic usage of meme lingo.

The bird market

Another view of the bird market

Selfie at the bird market. I had a theory that the guy glowering behind my left shoulder may have been a Taliban member who knew they were going to enter the city soon, and was wondering who was this Western retard.

As usual the streets were covered in a thick layer of orange-yellow sand. The main path we were on was at most eight feet at its widest sections, and the stalls to the sides were crowded with hundreds of birds in all kinds of metal, plastic, and wicker cages and containers. At one point we passed some metal-smiths using an angle grinder, with the sparks going right into the faces of the birds. They didn't react at all, and I reckoned they must have gone blind by now from staring at sparks for who knows how long. Seemed to me that however much these people undeniably loved their birds, sometimes there wasn't as much forethought as there could have been.

I had no idea that the Afghans were such avid ornithophiles. However, my guide soon started explaining the darker side to this place. Many of the birds were specifically bought and sold for fighting and could fetch high prices. In particular, my guide pointed out a native species of partridge that locals called *kowk*, which almost made me giggle. This fat, brown-gray bird slightly bigger than a pigeon apparently made a fierce fighter. Their combat was a highly popular form of entertainment. In addition to fighters, the Afghans also prized birds that were particularly beautiful specimens. Those who had a really nice bird could keep them in a cage on display at their home or business like a work of art to flex on the neighbors.

It occurred to me that this was basically Afghanistan's makeshift stock exchange. Unable to invest in national securities or bonds or any other kind of fractional ownership program, here the residents of Kabul were buying and selling birds in hopes of reselling them for a higher price at some later date.

The market seemed to go on forever in an endless maze of twists and turns. I became extra vigilant when my guide informed me that I should watch my pockets closely for thieves, as there were local troubled teens and pickpocketing was a major concern for foreigners in general.

I was on a mission in the back of my mind to buy an Afghan rug or two to sell online and hopefully recoup some of the cost of my trip. I figured there were bound to be collectors who would eat that stuff up.

However, this didn't seem like the place to do it, and frankly after a couple hours of browsing this unusual and enthralling place I was beginning to be tempted to buy a bird, so to save me from the consequences of that decision, Alem and I set off with his brother driving us to the next destination, which was a dam called Band-e Qargha directly west of Kabul. The dam formed a reservoir, a large, beautiful, baby-blue body of water that stretched for what seemed to me to be several miles. Standing near the shore, I gazed across the surface of the shimmering turquoise and toward the powerful, snow-capped mountains rising proudly in the distance on the other side. It was certainly not a sight I had expected to find in Afghanistan.

Nearby, there was a small but impressive traditionally constructed bridge that reached out into the water supported by stone columns, culminating in a small, sturdy-looking square building with calm blue walls and a metal roof of the same color. The sun beamed off of the metal, scattering glittering diamonds across the gentle lapping waves.

The blue building on the water

We walked across the bridge and into the small building's cool, dark interior, and Alem started telling me a tale or rumor about the king who had built the structure hundreds of years ago. I was trying to concentrate, when I was distracted by a few voices behind us and turned to see five or so nearby Afghan lads. They sounded angry and were clearly focused on us as they began to get closer, almost circling us. Naturally I couldn't understand a word they were saying, but I knew it wasn't good, and the way they were leaning in showed they definitely weren't looking for a fun conversation. I noticed they were also keeping their hands in their pockets and looked like they may have been holding something. If this was anything like London, I reasoned, then it was probably a knife, or at least they wanted me to think so, so I mirrored them, sticking my hands in my own pockets as if reaching for something and pretending I was also holding a knife hidden.

I looked to Alem, and he hastily explained to me under his breath that they were offended that we were speaking English and were saying that I should "go back to my country." *Based!* I thought. I myself was rather opposed to immigration in my home country. I certainly sympathized, but on the other hand the West was currently keeping their entire economy running, so I felt they didn't really have a leg to stand on here. In any case, I didn't feel like getting stabbed.

Alem and I walked right up to them and started forcefully shaking their hands. He began making up a story on the fly about how we were here on business, basically trying to complicate things as much as possible so that they would just leave us alone. A security guard standing nearby also took notice of the situation, and when they saw that they disgruntledly accepted our handshakes and then left with sullen glances.

I felt good about our quick thinking, but my guide was visibly shaken and started insisting that we leave immediately. I gathered that the interaction may not have been the last if we stayed, so we got back into the car and took a different route home to the safe house. When we got back, I started talking to Alem.

"Why were you so worried? Were those guys going to come back?"

He seemed to hesitate, somewhat uncomfortable about answering me. Finally, he did.

"They know that I work with the US. Lots of people around here don't like that. Some of them think people like me are collaborators, and so they hate us."

He went on to state that he felt it best we stay home for a bit now just to make sure that we weren't followed. I agreed; this was fine with me, and I certainly did not want him to come to harm on my account. It was a while since I'd eaten, so I grabbed one of the menus to plan a nice hearty takeaway. I was curious how the food I already knew differed from the version over here, so after looking it over, I settled on ice cream and some kebabs.

It arrived quickly, and I felt ashamed for the Uber Eats drivers back home who were easily outdone by the speed of the service in Kabul. I opened it, and the dishes were like nothing I'd seen before. Both kebabs and ice cream came in clay bowls with lids, decorated with neat patterns. As someone very much wary of ingesting microplastics, this was a definite improvement to the way I normally received my food. I checked the bottom of one of the bowls and saw that it was dated 2003. I thought about how some Afghan had made this almost two decades ago and they were just now using that part of their product supply.

The kebabs came with rice that was very well cooked, and the meat was rich, smokey, and tender with little crisp corners around the edges of the meat pieces. Overall, it was some of the best food I'd ever tasted. I was less keen on the Afghan ice cream. It was also very different and contained a spaghetti-like substance and was more akin to milk with transparent noodles and nuts, far removed from the solid, creamy goodness I was used to. It had the weirdest taste—I'm sure it was goat's milk—and it went straight through me. I drank some tap water, which in retrospect was probably unwise, to help get it down. The water did have an odd aftertaste but sufficed to wash down the sorry excuse for ice cream.

I had a full stomach now and the jetlag was beginning to catch up to me, so I decided to head to bed a little early so I could meet up with Alem early the next morning. First, I had a brief shower. The water pressure was pitiful, and the temperature was lukewarm, but honestly that felt

My delicious kebabs and my disappointing ice cream

welcome compared to the heat. I had actually been hoping to take a cold shower like I usually did at home, but that wasn't possible. It appeared that even domestic plumbing was not immune from the Afghan heat.

Upon climbing into the bed, I realized the mattress was absolutely rock hard, like a frozen marshmallow. Surprisingly, I found it very comfortable to sleep on and firm enough that I could get up easily in the morning without wanting to sleep in. During my time spent being homeless some years back, I'd grown accustomed to sleeping on the ground and hadn't regularly slept in a bed since. The mattress felt like the perfect in-between, and in a fit of inspiration I spent a few minutes Googling the import taxes from Afghanistan, but gave up after remembering that the airlines are wankers and would just screw me over in some way.

At that point I realized how funny my situation was. Here I was, an English physics student stressed out from working London investment banking internships, taking a break before graduation in Afghanistan of all places. I decided to post to the travel board of 4chan to share and let people ask questions. I was expecting at most two or three before the thread died because even though I certainly saw my trip as interesting, I really didn't think it was all that crazy.

How wrong I was. The thread blew up my phone with the replies, and after I successfully proved that I was really there with photos and such, people started going insane. I stayed up for several hours reading and replying, making new friends around the world who hung on every detail of my journey. People seemed to like my wording, my attitude, and my travel, so I thought maybe I could post more, and there were hundreds of replies within hours. Still, I was sure this notoriety would blow over once I woke up. I gave my new friends a virtual tour using zoom and fell asleep a few hours later, ready for another adventure in the morning.

August 14th
Adventure Awaits

A NEW DAY DAWNED AND A FRESH ADVENTURE BEGAN. I HAD BECOME well acquainted by now with inner city Kabul, and next I wanted to explore the outskirts. Kabul was undeniably foreign to me, but at the same time there were shadows of familiarity everywhere in the advertising signs, the occasional English, the cultural references, often out of date, but unmistakable. It felt like a weird mesh of Western commercialism with an organic, native culture with which it could never be reconciled. I wanted to see what the "real" Afghanistan was like outside, the part untainted by Westernization, the same flavor that I had felt hints of at the bird market.

I didn't know very much of the history of Western foreign policy toward Afghanistan. The only things that had stuck in my mind on the matter were surely just rubbish or propaganda passed down from our out-of-touch politicians, purposefully too opaque for the nation to understand or make use of, valuable only for justifying war or immigration or spending or whatever the current cause was. The wisp of a thought struck me, how my politicians' actions were nearly as divergent from my own interests as a British man, as my state's foreign policy toward Afghanistan seemed from the interests of the Afghan people.

I met Alem again in the sitting area of our lodging and we sketched out a plan for me to experience the Afghan countryside. As we were exiting the Green Zone our hotel was located in, I caught a glimpse of a mural painted on a wall made of concrete slabs. There were quite a few of these around the city. I had already seen others. Some of them were typical local scenes and pictures of smiling children and prosperous times, while others depicted events or individual people and had writing that I didn't understand, and which I assumed was often propaganda or political. This mural had, of all people, George Floyd, the American Black man who's rap sheet included gunpoint robbery of a pregnant woman, who's fentanyl related death while in police hands had recently sparked civil unrest across that whole country. My jaw fell open.

I quickly asked our driver to pull over, and we parked the car to get out and take a closer look. I was astonished that this was up on a wall in Kabul, and I was really curious if any of the locals actually knew who it was, so we asked a couple passers-by. One man shrugged and said he had no idea. Another told us he had assumed it was a picture of Obama, and one guy didn't understand at all as he had apparently never seen a Black man in his life. I learned later that after the Taliban had consolidated their takeover, they painted over all these murals as they were "Western symbols," including the one of George Floyd. Based!

Heading on our way again to the west, we passed by the Soviet Tank Graveyard, a place on the outskirts of the city where dozens of old Russian tanks and other military vehicles sat rusting in the sun. I thought it was a pretty cool sight, and also wondered if these were perhaps up for grabs, as it seemed that no one was really doing anything with them. With a reassembled zombie tank, I could become the most heavily armed man in England, which would certainly be a better use for one of these than lying in a ditch. I started Googling export laws again and what costs would go into transporting an aged Soviet military vehicle. Alas, I resigned myself to the fact that I could not airlift a tank. The three of us continued northward up the infamous Saricha Road on our way out of Kabul.

Markets lined the side of the road back-to-back for miles, all seemingly selling the same assortment of soda and fruit. I couldn't imagine how any of them made money because it seemed like all their prices and products were almost exactly the same. With the scarce amount of foot-fall they appeared to receive, it looked like they just sat there all day under the shade, hoping that someone would come along to buy some food. In areas where there was traffic, a child would sometimes run up and start hawking food from car window to car window, which did at least seem more convenient than Uber Eats.

On our way out of Kabul

Markets seen through one of the windshield stickers (above) and trash that was littered around the city (below)

The city had been covered by the acrid stench of raw sewage and battery acid, occasionally whisked about but never dispersed by gusts of dry wind. The small rivers or waterways that it appeared to rely on for drinking water were clogged with sun-bleached plastic bottles and other garbage. All of this changed dramatically as we reached the outskirts.

As we found ourselves farther away from the city, the frequency of the stands began to thin out and the scenery around us opened up to vast stretches of desert and wasteland, a tremendous, open expanse with nothing in sight in any direction apart from faint mountains stoically resting in the distance. The only other features were the occasional cattle herd, guided by men on donkeys, that I spotted off to the side or that blocked the road crossing with their livestock.

The road was truly atrocious, although I don't think it was necessarily the Afghans' fault. While I liked to joke about the roads in Western nations being terrible, in Afghanistan it was at the point that sometimes there simply was no road at all, and I'm not talking about a dirt track, but instead whole chunks of the road being completely gone. There were numerous sections where in the place of a good hundred feet of road there was just a massive, empty, three-foot-deep pothole. Cars were forced to go off the road to avoid it. It had to have been from bombing. I didn't ask Alem, but there was no other explanation in my mind.

Occasionally we would pass small settlements, if you could call them that. They were tiny groupings of dwellings, sometimes of what looked like stone or bricks blending into the sands, sometimes of corrugated metal or plywood. It almost seemed fake at times, like there couldn't possibly be anything in those places besides memories and lost threads of history washed away by the fiery sands, and yet I saw people there going about their business. I wondered what on earth they did in such a desolate area, and how often they saw others from outside their little village.

Sometimes it seemed like the settlements we saw really were just ruins, skeletons of sand and clay slowly blending back into the inexorable landscape from which they had been raised. They were surely hundreds of years old, and yet I wondered if they had ever seen a single tourist or archeologist. Information about these areas wasn't available online, and nobody other than the locals would have had memories of the history behind them. It felt weird to think how in the West, almost everything is documented and can be thoroughly researched by anyone with the autism to be interested, and meanwhile here entire generations of stories were reduced to whispers and one sentence summaries on Wikipedia. One image I saw that will stay with me for a long time is that of a bundle of mere wooden sticks, no bigger than ten by ten feet, which was being used as a *home* by a family of five people. Some children behind it seemed to be making bricks that they then baked in the sun. We had stopped briefly at that point, and I had already given away all the money that I brought as charity, so I just gave them the food that I had on me, and as we drove away, I prayed that their situation would improve.

One of the structures we passed

I saw extreme poverty in Afghanistan

As we traveled further from the city into the mountains, leaving behind the desert plains, the landscape changed again, and Afghanistan became a natural paradise. The toxic rivers of Kabul here became natural wonders of baby blue water, caressed by hills of undisturbed grass and sand. The road hugged imposing cliffs, and in the craggy rock faces there were nestled some of the most beautiful structures I've seen. Most of them were made again with the same stone, brick, or clay that blended into the landscape as though formed by God's hand or the eons of time, and some looked like they had been carved into the rock itself. The streams alternated between gently snaking currents and rapids rushing over rocks. I saw children playing in them, splashing each other and yelling happily, and on the cliffs, men sitting with their legs dangling over the edge, having a smoke while enjoying the majestic view.

The road wound dramatically up through the mountains, and in multiple places I saw signs that landslides were all too common here. There were spots where the road hadn't been fully cleared, or was clearly damaged. Above were the sloping mountain sides that may have recently donated some rock to the road below, or had the potential of doing so. I warily eyed a few looming outcroppings of loose stone as we passed beneath them.

Alem explained to me that landslides and huge, bombed-out potholes were not the only hazards. Particularly for roads that ran along rivers, water erosion also presented a concern. There would often be no way to know how much running water had eaten the ground beneath a road, or the road itself, until it simply collapsed.

At that point in my life, it was the hottest place I'd ever been to. The heat filled the air and all the space around us, and the sun beat down relentlessly. I got the impression that none of the vehicles in Afghanistan had a functioning air conditioning system; as a consequence, the windows were perpetually down. The wind was dry and added to the dehydrating effect of the sun. The beaches back home in England were my only point of comparison, but Afghanistan might as well have been another planet, this one rather closer to the sun.

On the road through the mountains

Despite all this, I thought about the possibility of living here. The natural beauty often distracted me from the harsh climate. I reasoned that the cost of living must be next to nothing, and I was sure I could get used to the heat, particularly with how comfortable the clothes were.

As we drove along, Alem told me more about what we were seeing. Many of the holes littered throughout the rock faces were abandoned mining caves, some of which now were being used as dwellings, including by wealthy residents of Kabul who converted them into alternative housing to escape the city. Wealthier people in the area had large villas painted with sun bleached pastel yellows and pinks, which included large, closed-off gardens filled with greenery, like their own personal Eden in the midst of Afghanistan's barren landscape.

We stopped at one of the gardens to walk around

Another view of the gardens

After the gardens, we resumed our journey and began talking about mountain climbing, which I knew as a popular sport in the West, and was curious how much it was done over here. The concept of climbing mountains for fun was beyond foreign to him, and not something in the mind of the average Afghan. The only comparison he had was for military training.

We were interrupted mid conversation by a military checkpoint. Several Afghan soldiers stood blocking the road, their vehicles parked close by. Their expressions were not friendly, and they wielded wood furnished AK-47s that looked like they were manufactured by the Soviets.

Two of them pointed their rifles at us, fingers on the trigger, with little regard for the norms of gun safety.

One of the men approached my window. I smiled winningly and whipped out my passport, holding it outside the car. He kept his guard up and asked what my reason was for coming to Afghanistan.

"Fun," I replied, trying to sound lighthearted but not too cheeky. It was the right answer apparently—amazing how much honesty gets you!

"Very good, Englishman." He cracked a smile and lowered his weapon, then took my passport and began flipping through it. I'm quite sure he wasn't even inspecting my visa but was just looking at the pictures of the queen inside.

The man spent a few minutes looking through the passport, occasionally glancing up at me. He handed it back and stated in a matter-of-fact way that made no attempt to conceal pride that he was a well-respected man in his village and he wanted to get a photo taken with me. I glanced at Alem, wondering if this was somehow a trap with an ulterior motive and I was about to be robbed, kidnapped, or extorted. However, I had said I was here for fun, and besides, he had the gun so I could scarcely say no. After taking a selfie with his seven-year-old Android and getting a firm handshake, we were allowed to continue down the road once more.

We were now in the beautiful Panjshir Valley. Alem told me that many of the people that lived in this area were Tajiks, one of Afghanistan's largest minority groups. The sparkling river snaked through the valley like a great serpent wrapping itself around the country, held in the gentle palm of the silent mountains.

After a few hours we stopped at a major local landmark. The road was winding up a mountain when I saw a large complex on the left.

"What is this place?" I asked him as he turned the car into the area.

"This is the tomb of the great military commander and martyr, Ahmad Shah Massoud. In the eighties, he helped defeat the Soviets and drive them out of Afghanistan. This area is where he came from. We call him the Lion of Panjshir."

I could hear the pride with which Alem spoke as he recounted the man's exploits. One thing I was curious about.

"You called him a martyr. Tell me, how did he die? Was it in battle against the Soviets?"

"No, he was martyred by Al Qaeda terrorists. They posed as journalists and killed him with a suicide bomb. Do you know when they did it?"

"No, I don't, was it a special date?"

"It was September 9th, 2001, just two days before 9/11. Because America invaded Afghanistan soon after, a lot of people see this as signifying the beginning of the era of American occupation."

There was so much more history to all of these events than I knew about as a Westerner.

We headed up the steps to the monument. Most of the area was built with a fancier, patchy, white-ish and gray stone that elevated it significantly in appearance over the structures I'd seen on the way. The complex appeared to be mid-construction. We stood in it for a while looking around. There was a large, open courtyard with columns on the sides but no walls and buildings on both ends, and there were clear signs of plans for fountains outside and an expanded royal style garden, as well as marble interiors for the main building. On the right was a hill with a large sort of open tower. This was the mausoleum of the martyr.

We went up to the monument through the building on the right. At the top floor, it opened up to the crest of the hill. Nearby, I saw more old Soviet tanks and military vehicles, many of which were painted with various colorful patterns of dotted lines. They were all behind a wire fence, and Alem told me that lots of children and tourists liked to try and climb on them, but there was an elderly man in one of the nearby villages who kept an eye on the tanks and fired off warning shots if he saw anyone not respecting the fence. Rumor has it that he served during the Soviet war.

The tower that the tomb was in was made of the same stone and style as the rest of the area. There was a walled glass interior on the first floor, and above that a large open space with four thick arches supporting the top. I couldn't tell if there was anything up there, but I didn't see a way of getting there, so it's probably just how the architect chose to design it.

The old Soviet vehicles

After taking in the view for a few moments, I realized I needed to use the bathroom. However, before I felt compelled to defile the sacred ground of a war hero, I fortunately discovered a portaloo on the edge of a cliff with a village in the distance. If there had been a particularly strong gust of wind at that moment, it could have really ruined the day of some poor man living below. Hopefully he didn't have a sunroof. Regardless of how vile it smelled inside, the fact that someone had cut out a giant window in the plastic, allowing me to overlook the valley, made this definitely the most scenic and awe-inspiring piss of my life. It may be the most dangerous, war-torn country on earth, but it was still more beautiful than anything I'd seen in bonny England.

My view while pissing

On the way back, we had to go down a one-way dirt track to recon-nect with the two-way road below. While we were doing this, we came across another armed checkpoint. I saw Alem's face darken with obvious fear and realized that there must be something different about this one and we were probably in some danger. As we slowed, I saw an armored vehicle with a turret on top with a large gun that was pointed toward us, tracking our approach. This was becoming a common theme in Afghan-istan. There was a bearded gentleman manning it who glowered as though he were projecting every tragedy in the country onto me specifi-cally. Two of the men sported black turbans, and I realized that these were Taliban.

We came to a stop respectfully as they surrounded the car. One of them approached my window like previously and addressed me in Eng-lish.

"Where are you going to?"

"We're driving home—"

"Home is England?" He cut me off before I could finish.

"Well yes, but we're hardly driving to England. I'm staying in Kabul."

"Ok, and what is your business here?"

"Fun," I replied without hesitation, handing him my tourism visa. He looked it over quickly, not seeming to care that much, and handed it back.

"Ok, just be careful, there are some bad men around here, very bad."

I took back my visa and at that point realized that the Taliban, a ter-rorist group, was telling me to be careful as there was something out there more dangerous than them. I glanced over at their armored vehicle. I saw the gentleman who was interrogating me catch my look, so I seized the opportunity without hesitation.

"Could I please take a picture in it?"

The man began chuckling to himself and started talking to the others in his language, presumably relaying what I had said. The rest of the Tal-iban also started chuckling wholeheartedly. He turned back to me.

"But I have not let you go yet, have I?"

"Because you're inviting me to climb on your vehicle?" I responded cheekily. Somehow this worked; I think he must have thought that I was simply too retarded to be a spy, especially since, as everyone knows, spies always travel on business visas anyhow.

He gave his permission, and I got out and started climbing. The men were all silent and watching, and I could tell they were judging me. After all, I'm sure they did not have the best impression of the British. I made it on top and sat in the gunner's seat, grasping the handles of the machine gun, and made a motion like I was shooting, which elicited some chuckles from the onlookers. Next, I pointed in the direction of my fake gunfire and yelled "Infidels!" The leader again translated to his people, and this time they erupted into laughter. I smiled, and it appeared that I had won their approval, at least to an extent. Good thing that I hadn't fired for real, because the machine gun was loaded without a safety, and I'm sure that if I'd accidentally shot up a village of war heroes, they would not have been nearly as amused.

Sitting on top of the Taliban vehicle

After taking a fantastic selfie, I climbed down, and the atmosphere was a lot more relaxed. I shook the hand of each man, and they relayed to me through their translator to tell good things about their nation when I went home, which I gladly confirmed that I very much intended to do. To my surprise, they went so far as to invite me to their place for tea, which for the British at least is the equivalent of inviting a stranger for a pint at the pub. Before I accidentally joined the Taliban, Alem, who still appeared uneasy about the situation, reminded them and me that it was growing dark and we needed to head back.

One of my favorite pictures from the trip

The evening was arriving, and a fog had descended. As we continued down the dirt road, I saw pretty much the only thing that could still have surprised me that day. There were some people ahead, and the shape of one of them stood out from the rest, as it was clearly someone not wearing local clothing. As the fog cleared, I saw boots, and as we approached closer realized that they were in fact yellow and black Dr. Martens. I stared and joked out loud about whether a White woman had somehow wandered into Afghanistan. Then we drove up and saw her face, and I realized that indeed, a White woman had somehow wandered into Afghanistan.

There was no question about not stopping to talk to her, so as we slowed, I leaned out the window to say hi. She seemed friendly and also stopped when she saw us and smiled. She stood about six feet tall with light blonde hair, white skin, and lovely green eyes and was somehow wearing leather shoes and a biker jacket despite the sweltering heat.

I asked her name but couldn't pronounce it back, so I guessed that she must be Polish because their language is nonsense. It turned out that she had been traveling from the age of twenty-four and had already made her way across the entire Middle East and was now going through Asia with nothing more than a bicycle. She had come into Afghanistan through Pakistan. Upon hearing this, I joked that I also avoided airlines at all costs, which made her laugh. Unfortunately, she did not speak much English, which got me thinking. She couldn't speak any Dari or Pashto, the main languages of Afghanistan. I had no doubt that I was currently talking with the only Polish-speaking person in the entire country.

We supplemented our English with some hand gestures to communicate our intended directions. I pointed to the back seat to offer her a lift, but she gestured in the opposite direction, toward the front lines of the war. At this point I knew that she was protected by God and wanted to see what would happen, so there was no point in warning her, as she clearly understood where she was. I got her number on Whatsapp, and the next minute I watched as she cycled away from us toward the sunset. *Future wife*, I thought to myself.

I pulled my head back into the car, and we set off back to the hotel for the night. As the sun set in beautiful shadows and colors on this excellent day, I slumped into the sandy car seat and fell asleep with the *Lawrence of Arabia* soundtrack playing in my head.

A picture I took for my girlfriend back home

August 15th
Taliban Takeover

SUNDAY, AUGUST 15TH, 2021 WAS THE DAY THAT EVERYTHING CHANGED. I
went to sleep the night before with no definite plans. I woke up to the
news that the Taliban had just issued an ultimatum to the US-backed
Afghan government, demanding that they surrender Kabul by 4:00 p.m.,
otherwise the Taliban would take it by force. Alem and I both knew I had
to get out as soon as possible. The jig was up. I may have made some
friends at the checkpoint outside of the city, but I had no reasonable ex-
pectation of being able to leave the country alive if the Taliban seized the
capital city and, more importantly, the airport. As soon as he heard the
news, he started speeding to my hotel, bringing along a knowledgeable
local driver. The news of the Taliban's ultimatum had not yet hit the general population, and we hoped to get out ahead of it and get going while
movement was still possible, before the panicked congestion got too bad.

I was wandering around the courtyard of the hotel, somewhat per-
turbed but patient, when the demanding buzz of my cell phone startled
me from my reverie. I saw Alem's name on my screen and answered eagerly, hoping for good news.

"I'm going to be late," he informed me. "Traffic in the city is gridlocked for miles." I nodded inadvertently while talking as if he were in
front of me. No surprise there and no need to let it add to my worry. I
already knew traffic was notoriously congested, and the brief respite of
the Friday holiday was over.

In ordinary circumstances, the busy streets could be expected to crawl along in a decent imitation of the New York or LA daily grind, but during a country-wide panic caused by the imminent arrival of the all-but-victorious insurgency, it was a parking lot. The Taliban advance had been far faster and more efficient than anyone had predicted. Alem had told me that over the past weeks, refugees from all over the country fleeing the Taliban had been trickling into the city, but now with the news that Kabul itself was threatened, it was becoming a flood that added to the already impressive clog of transportation and frequently slowed down cars to below a walking pace. It was not unusual for walking to be markedly faster than the automotive alternative, and people would sometimes alternate between riding in a car and continuing their journeys on foot. We would soon be joining them.

I wrapped up my phone call and sat down to await Alem and the driver's arrival. I wanted to convince them to take me downtown to get money out of the ATM before I left so that I could distribute it to the newly arrived refugees from the neighboring provinces. *For all the good it will do,* said a voice in the back of my head. But still, it's what I had come to do in the first place, and even if I could just give charity to a few it would surely help them in some way, whether purchasing food or perhaps bribing favors out of soldiers or militants. There was little I could do besides that other than entrust their lives into God's hands, much as my own already was. Kabul was falling. The only question was when.

Alem arrived with his brother, and they both acquiesced to my plan. As we stepped out of the relative cool of the garden, the arid heat hit me in the face. Its now familiar shroud, strangely comforting, helped calm my nerves amid the notable increase in frantic activity and tension I felt around us on the street. There was no mistaking or ignoring the universal atmosphere of nervous anticipation. As we slid open the heavy metal door that had sheltered me, I saw that the park on the opposite side of the street had become a refugee town overnight. Where previously there had been a few, now the whole area was covered with a patchwork of ragged, torn, and dusty tents pitched in no particular pattern. Displaced Afghans sat or stood at the makeshift dwellings that now constituted their only earthly homes, watching their children wander around similarly aimlessly. I felt a sharp pang of sympathy for them. Though families were around them, and their parents were there, even they could not provide a source of familiarity in the present circumstance of their world having been turned on its head. I saw the adults occasionally glancing in the direction of the city's outskirts, surely wondering when their brethren and soon-to-be conquerors would arrive.

Our drive didn't last long. Conceding to the gridlocked streets, we got out of the car and Alem told the driver to meet us near the central banking area with the car. We would be faster on foot and with any luck would be able to grab money from the ATM and then hop right back in the vehicle and stay moving.

We walked for about forty minutes into downtown Kabul through the throngs of natives and refugees and found that the news of the Taliban advance had preceded us. Hundreds of people with the same idea were already flocking around the ATMs. One look was all it took to realize that I had no hope of using it myself. As we arrived at the square, the manic chorus of cell phone alerts erupted into a crescendo of shouting and panic from the crowd. My guide and I both instinctively looked down at our own phones and instantly saw what was causing the clamor. The announcement of the Taliban's 4:00 p.m. deadline had just hit social media.

We took one look at the size of the desperate crowd separating us from the few ATMs and knew that the money in them would be gone in a matter of minutes. At one point yesterday, I had drained one ATM by withdrawing only $200 USD. Today, the top one percent of the city's economic classes was attempting to withdraw their entire life savings, to say nothing of the rest who surely also wanted to grab anything they had for the meager security it provided. As the consequences of the confirmed deadline dawned on them, the full implication of the Taliban's ultimatum struck. With one mind, the Afghan urbanites realized that this could be their last chance to access their bank accounts and credit lines. We stood watching them frantically push and shove each other in front of the banks. They knew that the person in front of them might be the one to take the last dollar from the machine's slot or teller's drawer. Curses and anguished supplications to Allah filled the air. Desperate people banged on the ATMs, praying that if they tried the machine one more time, the money they needed would come out. There was no hope to be found here.

Placing a hand on my arm, Alem drew my attention away from the spectacle to tell me that he had just learned that our driver had managed to extricate himself from traffic and was available to continue our journey. He had apparently done a loop around the main roads and was saying that he would meet us in the direction of downtown. At this point, the severity of the situation was becoming manifest in the behavior of the city's occupants. We knew what the news had been from around the country over the past few days, but, at least for myself, this was the first time I had been confronted with a raw example of human panic affecting my ability to operate. While the money itself wasn't an immediate concern, the experience brought my current situation into focus. I was no better off than the rest of these people, especially if I wouldn't be able to find a way out of the country by normal means.

We kept moving. Alem was still somewhat skeptical that the situation was as dire as the bank runners perceived it to be. As we hurried along to meet the driver, he told me of how false alarms that incurred similar responses had been quite common over the last few months, amplified by digital news outlets. Afghanistan was no stranger to hysterical journalism accelerated and intensified by social media. His words did help to ease my mind.

Among the fleeing crowds, I saw a group of young boys chase each other down the street in front of us, pushing one another and knocking over produce stands and anything else that happened to be in front of them, provoking outrage and oaths from the sellers. A father or an uncle grabbed one of the boys by the arm and shook him roughly, demanding he behave himself. The castigated youngster then fell back into line with his family with the mildest of chastised looks, belying his youthful intuition that the adults were no longer in control.

Pictures of the bank run

Blissfully unconcerned with the panic around them, older residents of the city were laying down in the middle of the sidewalks to sunbathe, peacefully spreading blankets over the dust and concrete. In their defiant stoicism, they demanded space from the fleeing refugees, most of whom respectfully moved aside despite their mad dash. When they didn't, there were consequences. I saw an old man who looked nearly asleep grab the ankle of an unfortunate passerby who carelessly stepped too close. Crashing to all fours and indignantly yanking himself free, the refugee cursed his prone assailant. Hacking intermittently from the dust kicked up by his victim, the older man laughed heartily and with a final satisfying cough rolled over to get a better angle for the warm rays.

As we walked past a row of shops, we noticed the owners making the most of the situation, increasing or decreasing prices for maximum benefit from every interaction. People turned into preppers, trying to hoard as much food as they could and sell off what was perishable. Basic goods like water and other necessities were suddenly worth their weight in gold, while luxuries were bartered away at fire-sale prices. I spied a middle-aged shopkeeper with a dark gray vest haggling intensely with some bystanders and remembered seeing him among the crowd at the ATM queue earlier, trying to withdraw money. Evidently unsuccessful, he was now selling his watches for pennies on the dollar in an attempt to extract some lifeboat cash in a sinking city. It looked grim, but I still wished him the best. His was a common scene we would pass by many times that day. It reminded me of what it was probably like on Wall Street in 2008, when the hedge fund managers all realized that their assets were worthless.

Items that were previous indications of status were now dispensed with as though they held the plague. In particular, everyone was trying to sell their Western clothes, anticipating that the Taliban weren't too keen on foreign drip. I had people practically shoving eighties-style jeans in my face, and it was kind of darkly funny to see what out-of-date (by Western standards) clothes had just been in vogue in Afghanistan.

A few people got so desperate that they dispensed with the normal pleasantries of commercialism entirely. We saw several ransacked stores, the owners either having given up on protecting their merchandise or having fled themselves.

About this time, the sweltering midday heat was reaching its full volume, and I became even more grateful for the comfy Afghan clothes. There was nothing to do other than press on.

Finally, sometime around 11:00 or 11:30 a.m. we met up with our driver again along one of the main roads. Having gotten thoroughly fed up with the local traffic, he abandoned the previous car and instead walked to his family members to use theirs, which was closer to us. We all clambered into a nondescript street car with the dust markings and paint scuffs of a local vehicle. In the midst of the urgency and commotion, we paused to plan our next steps.

The driver didn't want to go through the downtown area again. Alem agreed and explained the situation to me. "The main roads will all be full of these people running around. We should drive around the city and get back to the hotel that way."

He looked at me. I had no way of knowing if our luck would be any better along the new route, so I took their word for it and nodded. "That sounds good. let's go."

We drove toward the outskirts of the city. Our route went up a large hill, from where we could see down below into the city. Kabul is surrounded by mountains, and our plan was to loop around in a kind of triangle shape, almost exiting the city but not quite, in order to avoid the congestion in the center and enter from a different angle. My Afghan companions estimated that this should take less than half an hour. We were feeling invigorated by our resourcefulness and renewed sense of control over our circumstances, and were thoroughly unprepared for what happened next.

I was seated in the front passenger seat, with Alem in the back. As we crested the hill, the driver abruptly slammed on the breaks. Since seatbelts are a foreign custom in Afghanistan, we all jolted forward with a yell, and I put out my arm just in time to stop myself from face-planting directly into the dashboard. Alem and I looked up through the dust we'd kicked up ahead of us to see what had so violently interrupted our journey, and I got my second glimpse of the Taliban.

Several black Toyota pickup trucks kitted out with mounted machine guns in the beds were driving toward us, bearing black balaclava-clad fighters wielding AK-47s while the unmistakable white flags with the Shahada snapped in the wind behind them. When they saw us, they sped up and began shouting and gesturing, pointing their battle-worn rifles in our direction.

"Turn! Drive! Drive! Fast!" Everyone in the car yelled in both languages, and we needed no translators to know what each other was saying. With a skillful handbrake maneuver straight out of an urban action film, the driver swerved and pressed the accelerator to the floor, briefly breaking the front tires loose. My heart pounded as the adrenaline coursed through my veins.

The Taliban forces were now only a few minutes from the city. They had made it clear early in their campaign that they wanted a bloodless transfer of power, so an outright slaughter was seemingly off the table. Nevertheless, we knew that each pocket and clique of the mujahideen frequently acted on its own discretion, and there was no telling what might trigger a firefight, or what would happen if we fell into the hands of the fleet of technicals.

Driving away from the Taliban

As we returned to the bottom of the mountain, our hearts sank. The traffic was even worse than before, oozing out of every side street and alleyway. Futile car horns blared stochastically, but no one was getting anywhere fast. Some drivers would pull out guns and fire into the air in hopes of scaring others into merging or letting them through. The transportation infrastructure in Afghanistan leaves much to be desired, and the lack of many traffic lights and road signs certainly wasn't helping to maintain orderly driving conventions. Complicating the situation further were the drivers who had taken their cars onto the sidewalks to try and bypass the gridlock, ultimately doing nothing but worsening the congestion. Ever enterprising, some local merchants took advantage of the situation by walking through the traffic, selling their wares from car to car. We realized the situation was completely hopeless when we noticed that increasing numbers of motorists were simply abandoning their cars in the middle of the roads, creating an impassable blockade. Children could be heard crying over the honking as their parents dragged them through the mixture of human and automotive traffic.

Trying to make our way through the traffic

As we drove, I tried shortening the plan by buying a new plane ticket online in order to simply cut out the safehouse trip. In the original plan for the holiday, I wasn't due to leave until the 22nd, and even after the Taliban cut this short, I foolishly delayed buying a new ticket because I loath to spend the money and hated the fact that I had to leave so early. If I hadn't waited till the last minute, a lot of time would have been saved. If I had bought them before I left that morning, I would likely have also had the forethought to take all my stuff with me, which had slipped my mind. Now, I had neither tickets nor my other belongings, although I did have my passport with me.

I soon discovered that at this point it was too late. All my attempts resulted in my card being declined. I knew I wasn't short on funds, so I found myself in the surreal situation of messaging my bank's customer service to explain that there was a very real potential I would be beheaded by the Taliban if I couldn't get my card working. I laughed out loud when they bothered asking if I wanted to stick around to answer their customer satisfaction survey. After attempting the card again, I realized that the problem likely wasn't on my end but with the airline website. The mass surge in activity and attempted ticket purchases likely triggered some form of fraud prevention mechanism in their system and had halted all purchases. I amused myself for a moment by reflecting on the temptation to shell out the £19.99 life insurance policy that was an option with the ticket. If I was to die, at least I'd die lining my friends' pockets.

As a sidenote, when I originally got my tickets there was an option to buy terrorism insurance for just around £4, and apparently it counted cancelations due to terrorism as well. When I remembered this about a month after returning to England, I claimed and got the original ticket price back plus around twenty to thirty percent. Since the return ticket cost significantly more than the original outbound ticket, I basically recovered the cost of transportation, making my trip to Afghanistan essentially free.

At that time, I gave up trying to buy the ticket, and after a brief consultation we agreed that there was nothing for us to do but follow suit with the refugees abandoning their cars and get moving on foot before the army surrounding the city arrived in earnest. We ditched our car once again and set off at a light but urgent jog, leaving Alem's brother with the vehicle as he didn't want to lose it. I wouldn't see him again.

After getting out of the car, we moved to the sidewalk, and I noticed off to the side a large ditch past which was an area where throngs of refugees had set up tents as temporary housing. The scene was reminiscent of the park outside my hotel but on a much larger scale. The residents milled about in listless agitation.

We passed a car that had crashed face first in the ditch. I paused my jog briefly to look closer and confirm what happened to the passengers. There were two people inside, their bodies covered in blood and slumped over the wrecked interior. Through the cracked window I could see their eyes frozen open in death. The air around was acrid with the smells of burning plastic, poor quality diesel, less-than-fresh fruit from the surrounding tent city, and now death. I noticed Alem motioning that we must hurry on. I glanced back at the wrecked car for a moment and swiftly crossed myself to pay my respects, then tore myself from the scene and kept running alongside my companion through the streets of Kabul.

On the way we saw other cars that had crashed into buildings, lampposts, and food stands. I couldn't stop to investigate them all, so I could only hope that they were just the result of people being in a real hurry to get out and not fatal accidents.

We had previously learned that the Taliban had inserted teams of militants among the general population, spreading through the entire city. The thought of this now briefly entered my mind as we ran. Our danger wasn't only from the encroaching army. Who knows what the Taliban sleeper cells would be emboldened or see fit to do now that their victory was in sight.

We had now entered into a denser area of the city. I kept my head down as we wove in and out of the crowds. In addition to not wanting to be recognized or stand out as a European, I also needed to keep my eyes on my feet to avoid the constant ground level obstacles before us. The sidewalk, like much of Kabul's infrastructure, was in significant disrepair, with gaping holes, large cracks, and dislodged pavers strewn everywhere. Occasionally, we had to move around or jump over a body lying in the way. I couldn't help but begin to agonize a bit over the fact that this obstacle course was adding precious seconds to our trip. I thought back to the sight of the Taliban trucks on the hill and the weather-worn men standing in the bed next to their flag and pushed forward with renewed vigor.

The plan at this point was to go back to the hotel so I could gather my essential belongings. After that we would go to the British embassy, as we'd been told online that the staff would remain there until 4:00 p.m. in accordance with the Taliban's announcement. I was relying on that to hold true so that I could be evacuated with them. A quick glance at my watch showed that it was about noon. In theory, we had roughly four hours.

We came across a still-open market stand selling clothes, and I quickly exchanged some cash for a burka to don as a disguise. My hope was that this would be sufficient to protect me from being instantly singled out by any Taliban agents. My conspicuously white skin would still have given me away if someone had looked closely, but I hoped that in the rush no one would scrutinize a fleeing "woman" so much. I don't have much of a girlish figure and was quite glad that these Sunni fundamentalists dressed their women rather differently than I was used to.

After another half an hour of alternated jogging and speed-walking, Alem and I were both exhausted. Our breaths came heavy, especially mine, and the temperature was affecting my head, which was probably exacerbated by the fact that it had also been a while since I'd had something to eat or drink. I coughed rust-colored sputum from the dust kicked up by the masses of people. My full body black burka Muslim housewife costume was not helping either. I was quite dehydrated and quickly becoming disillusioned with the crossdressing ruse. However, I reminded myself of the cross that rested around my neck and how all of this trial was a part of God's plan. If He wanted me dead then it would be for good reason, and if I was to struggle and survive then I must endure and stay faithful and trust Him. I calmed my thoughts and said a quick prayer thanking God for all of the blessings up to this point. The action helped me focus and gave me peace. I smiled underneath my face covering for the whole rest of the jog. Perhaps it was just an adrenaline high, but throughout most of this experience I wore a smile. I certainly hadn't expected to wake up and roleplay a *Metal Gear Solid* game that day.

As if in answer to my unspoken prayers, we saw some elderly people kindly putting out buckets full of water with a plastic cup attached to a piece of string. Afghanistan didn't observe many coronavirus precautions. Gratefully, we each took a quick sip and carried on. I saw other people dunking their whole heads in the buckets and the elders smacking them with a broom.

All around us were signs of a city collapsing. I watched Afghan soldiers in military uniform running for their lives and throwing their weapons into a dirty stream. I didn't understand the language, but the sentiment of every-man-for-himself translated just fine. Push had come to shove. We would be getting no help from them.

Part of what was helping us navigate at this point was the blimp. The US kept a massive, white blimp suspended over the center of Kabul. How, I don't know, and neither did any of the locals I asked. However, it was useful because you could see it from basically anywhere, and you would always know what direction you were coming from based on which advertisements you saw on the side. If you were going east to west, you would see an energy drink. This was really helpful since, especially to my untrained eyes as a Westerner, Kabul felt like a maze as the buildings and shops all looked very similar.

I finally decided to bite the bullet and abandon the burka. It certainly wasn't helping me stay cool, unlike the other Afghan clothes, and the hem reached to below the ankles, interfering with my ability to run. I didn't feel like tripping over myself at such a sensitive time, and besides, if I was going to die it might as well be with whatever was left of my dignity intact. Alem, who was always very concerned and serious about my safety, generously gave me a headscarf that I wrap around my head to lower my profile a little bit.

My disguise

Finally, after another half an hour, we arrived back at the area of the hotel. We rushed up to the metal outer gate and started knocking urgently. In a couple minutes, it turned to banging on the metal. I tried shouting so that my voice would be recognized. We knew that this is probably one of the most secure non-government buildings in the city, so the skepticism was understandable, but we had no other options. I stepped back and squinted at the barbed wire fence, then turned to Alem.

"Do you think there's a way of getting over this fence? If I did that, I could at least unlock the first door."

"You'd need something to protect you from the wire."

I glanced around and thought of the various market stands in the vicinity. "What if I buy a rug and throw it over?"

"If you did that, could you get in the house?"

I paused. Even if I scaled the wall, the second door was likely also locked, and so this could just result in me getting trapped. I shook my head, abandoning the idea. At a loss, we next began to contemplate sliding my passport underneath the door so that the inhabitants would know it's me. Just as we'd decided to abandon this risky plan, the fearful owner finally and unexpectedly swung the door open.

We rushed in, and I flew past the still peaceful, pristine garden and ran up three flights of stairs to pack my bags.

"I'll only take a few minutes!" I shouted to Alem. I packed everything I could, but without the time to neatly fold my clothes, I had to leave a few things behind. When clearing the bathroom, I noticed that my toilet was still clogged from the last time I'd used it and had been unable to flush. I laughed at the thought that this was the Taliban's problem now. I wheeled my suitcase downstairs and through the door, with both of us thanking the owners profusely and hurrying out.

As we were leaving through the garden, I looked up and noticed construction workers on top of one of the buildings next to us. It was a bit taller than most in Kabul, about six stories, and looked like it would eventually be apartments. There were several workers chilling on top. Some were working with a hammer or drill while others appeared to just be relaxing and watching the scenes playing out on the streets below, casually chatting and occasionally pointing and laughing. It was a funny contrast to see how people in Kabul could react so differently to their situation. Some were running around like mad, while others seemed resigned and unfazed, like these workers or the old men sunbathing earlier.

I took a moment in the garden to breathe. At that point I had everything I needed to flee the country, the embassy was less than a ten-minute walk, and the sight and smell of the garden was a welcome break from the chaos outside.

We went back out onto the street, and I realized that the distinct sound of my luggage wheels was liable to turn heads. Thankfully though people were too preoccupied to pay much attention. A group of orphan girls no older than ten years walked up to us crying and began pulling at our clothes. Alem told them to get somewhere safe, and we both gave them some money to buy enough food for a few nights. It broke our hearts knowing we couldn't do more, but we didn't have the cash to sustain ourselves beyond a day at most, and although theoretically we didn't have much farther to go, at this point I didn't want to take any chances.

Walking up to the embassy we immediately noticed that something was very wrong. The doors were open and there were locals walking in and out carrying stuff. Two guys who were carrying a large, ornate, beige sofa into a truck stopped for a second and looked embarrassed as they saw me. They must have thought I was one of the embassy staff. They soon continued though, and no one else really paid us mind. Alem inquired and told me that the embassy staff had abandoned it hours ago. There was no help to be found here. We were subsequently informed that this was likely the case for every other embassy as well.

The airport was our last shot. We looked through our messages for information for a moment just in case there was something that could help us. Upon checking my phone, I discovered I had hundreds of messages stating to go to the airport as there were ambassadors waiting there to meet up with citizens.

We broke into a jog again, now with the added encumbrance of having to drag my luggage across the bumpy streets and swing it along over the many cracks and ditches. Several strangers showed me random acts of kindness. One man helped me reapply my headscarf in such a way that it didn't become untangled as I walked. Another man, realizing where we must be headed, stopped to give us directions without even asking. The phone networks were impossibly slow at this point due to the high volume of usage, so we took people who gave directions at their word and carried on moving for over an hour.

We held out our hands a few times for hitchhiking, as we'd seen a few people get lucky that way. Sweetening the deal, we waved some cash, and a family with a vehicle stopped to pick us up. It was an extremely tight fit for all seven people in their small 1970s four-seater sedan, with their children crammed into the trunk. We got as far as we could until we hit the same gridlocked traffic as before, so we got out and pushed through the crowd. At last, we made it to the airport. There was a throng of people around, with lots of confusion and shouting. Five or six people immediately in front of us were roughly turned away by security. I heard the word "ticket" shouted in several different languages and realized that anyone without flights was being barred from entry. I waved my old ticket and passport in the air and got through the entrance with Alem.

There were young children selling masks at the security entrance. When they saw me, their faces lit up and they got really enthusiastic and crowded around, thinking they would sell more to a Westerner. I was really concerned for their safety and about the fact that they were here alone, but Alem shooed them away, telling them sternly to go home to their parents.

There were a few ANA soldiers in the area who still seemed committed to guarding the airport and providing some kind of order. I saw them questioning people and making some effort to make sure everyone had tickets and no one was bringing weapons. Two of them came up to us and started questioning me. As I started explaining my circumstance, much to my confusion they became very excited and started to shake my hand. They talked with Alem and he explained that they had been following my story on 4chan, which became a particularly surreal moment in an already surreal experience. After they patted us down and scanned our bags, we continued forward toward my terminal. The inside of the airport was weirdly calm. It struck me that this was like the eye of a hurricane.

When we entered the main terminal, we were immediately confronted by another guard who informed us that flights had been grounded. Most if not all of the diplomats had already left. Alem was told by the guard that only I could pass because I had a ticket. He tried his best to sweet-talk the man, telling him that I don't speak the language so it would be advantageous for me if he was there to help communicate with staff to find any remaining diplomats or Western soldiers. I had no idea what he was saying until later, but I knew Alem as a God-fearing man and trusted him completely throughout the whole ordeal. He got permission from the guard to proceed, so I waited for him to return in the same area of the airport where I first met him as he picked me up on my first day in the country. He came back twenty minutes later with some bad news: nobody was left. We were on our own.

We milled about the airport entrance for a while, mingling with some of the staff standing outside, both grateful for the company and hoping to glean some useful information. They seemed as much at a loss as we were for what to do next, and their conversation was colored with both horror and bewilderment as they discussed the timeline of what had happened. What they had expected to take months had occurred within minutes. Everyone agreed the situation was screwed up, and we took turns marveling and how it could have gone so bad so quickly. When I had woken up that day, Kabul was still a free city, administered by a government that had spent the past twenty years being supported and nurtured by the greatest military power on earth. Now, within hours, the mantle of power had passed to a very different group with hardly a shot being fired. Kabul, and all of Afghanistan, had passed from West to East. Without having left its borders, I was now standing in a completely different country. However, by the grace of God, I was alive and that was all I could afford to think about at that moment.

With a half-hearted irony, I pointed to an ATM near the doorway close to where we were standing. "Is there any chance that has cash in it?"

One of the Afghans laughed. "That one ran dry weeks ago!"

Evidently there were people who had not been nearly as surprised by the recent series of events, or maybe were just extra paranoid and in this case it paid off. Kabul's jet-setting class had clearly prepared themselves well beforehand.

The adrenaline was wearing off now, and the scalding sun and thick heat beating down on us increasingly called our attention to their presence. Alem and I found ourselves simultaneously tired, starved, parched, and sunburnt after hours of sometimes literal running around Kabul. We exchanged a worried glance. After all that, we remained no closer to our goal.

With a sigh, we both agreed that back at the hotel was the best place to wait out whatever was to come. Saying farewell to our airport friends, we began walking slowly back the way we had just come. The panicked frenzy of the past hours had begun to subside, and the city was turning quiet. The occasional yelling and clamor now felt like an imposition. The reason seemed apparent whenever the air was punctuated with gunshots. The Taliban must have entered without much resistance, as the city, for all intents and purposes, had surrendered. The panic of man was becoming replaced with the careless chirping of birds.

Still, there were signs of tragedy all around. We saw women weeping at the airport fences, staring through the wire at us and the other people denied exit from the country. We could see in their faces that they knew if *we* were unsuccessful, they had little to no hope themselves.

Jumping back over the security checkpoint barrier, I noticed that the plant watering hoses were still running, dispensing precious hydration. Ripping one from the garden bed, Alem and I took turns gulping down the dirty water and filling up our bottles. *Just like home,* I thought, reflecting on the off-color, fluoride laden, London tap water to which I was accustomed.

Despite the brief reprieve from debilitating dehydration, we were still physically and emotionally drained from the hours spent running around just to have to backtrack. The area where we were standing smelled of rubble. Nearby, the wreckage of a car was embedded in a concrete wall near the airport entrance, and I noticed a still body lying inside, the skin looking bloodless and drained of life. At this point such a scene had become an unfortunately common sight, and after saying another quick prayer, we kept moving.

During the whole ordeal, whenever I could, I would check in with the people following my story online from my 4chan posts. I saw everyone pleading for us to stay at the airport, but for me and my guide at the time it felt like the wrong move. Something in my gut told me that it wouldn't be safe, and with no food or clean water available, it wouldn't end well for us.

A few seconds later we ran into a familiar sight. Six or so Taliban trucks were rolling up along the road, and I recognized them as the same ones that had chased us coming over the mountain. The men were smiling and shouting to each other, reveling in their victory. The Afghan army had surrendered and let them through the gate onto the airport grounds, the final territory of their country that had not been captured. When they saw me, the mounted guns pointed in my direction, not explicitly but out of general caution at seeing a Westerner, and I suddenly realized that my headscarf was off and my cross was on top of my shirt and on full display. They were likely wary of the same news we had just recently seen, that of Western soldiers at the airport.

With all these observations running through my mind in quick succession, I simply said "screw it" and walked right out into the road in front of them. Cutting in front of the first truck, I tapped on the front to say "we're just passing" and gave the driver a thumbs up and the guys with AK-47s hanging off the truck a subtle nod. For a brief second, I blocked the Taliban's victory. Taken aback, they looked at each other confused, but one Taliban member cracked a smile at me and laughed. A horn sounded from the truck farthest in the back that couldn't see what was going on and was confused by the sudden stop.

"Alright, alright," I yelled, and gave them a thumbs down as I walked past. At this point, I felt past caring, and the gravity of my actions would only hit me when I thought about it later.

As we strode through the streets of Kabul, my senses were assaulted by the manifestations of ruin, rotting fruit and meat littering the sidewalks, cars abandoned in the street, yellowy brown dust sitting in the air. All the shops were closed. I could see elders still sunbathing in the streets, unmoved from where they were before the Taliban had assuredly passed them. I respected them.

Alem and I paused for a moment, surveying the scene and our current situation. We'd found our way here; now we had to go all the way back through the maze, and who knew what other obstacles would be in our path. Alem knew the direction roughly, but we hadn't come by a normal driving route. We looked at each other.

"Any ideas, mate?" I asked.

"We should keep moving. It's better if we look like we're going somewhere. It will look suspicious if we're standing around."

We decided that in any case if we kept walking, we would get *somewhere*, and with a bit of luck Alem should be able to find our way back. As we continued down the road, I thought of how many buildings that looked like copies of each other were now distinguished by differing designs of bullet holes.

Up ahead we saw four Taliban fighters and kept our heads down and pace even, hoping to just pass by unnoticed. However, they were on alert and two of them approached to intercept us. Both wore black turbans and carried AKs. One was also wearing beige body armor, presumably pinched at some point from a dead ANA or Western soldier, and a walkie talkie. He looked like he was LARPing as G.I. Joe, although I decided not to tell him that.

Alem started talking with them in their language, and I was cut out from understanding what was going on. Then he was dismissed and I suddenly became the centerpiece. It turned out that the Taliban members wanted to speak with me. In broken English, they asked me where I was from. Ironically, I understood them better than some of the accents from Birmingham.

I put on a slight charming grin. "I'm from Wales."

They stared at me in confusion. "What's Wales?"

"It's a small country, and they hate the British."

The Taliban looked at each other and erupted into laughter. Apparently satisfied by the bad-mouthing of Britain, they seemed to conclude that I was all right and shook my hand before walking away.

Wandering further, we spotted a group of White people and decided that the best thing to do would be to just follow them, as they seemed to know where they were going. Sure enough, upon turning a corner we came upon a crowd of twenty or so people clustered around the entrance of a compound. It had the feeling of a small castle, with large walls about four meters tall. Barbed wire coils snaked across the top, watched by the vigilant electronic eyes of security cameras. I noticed a few spots where what looked like rags of clothing were tangled in the wire. *God only knows what happened there*, I thought. With the thick walls and security, it definitely looked like a safehouse or military asset, though I found out later that it had originally been a hotel. There were red Turkish flags with the white crescent and star.

Pushing our way toward the front, I waved my British passport and was greeted by the Turkish troops, who seemed to speak minimal English but enough to inform me that the safehouse wasn't for me.

"I said British, not Greek," I joked, and saw one of them crack an involuntary smile. Still, they didn't appear willing to budge on their policy.

Alem began speaking, and he and I argued back and forth with the soldiers in both languages for a few minutes. Our persistence paid off, not due to any success of our abilities of persuasion, but because it turned out that there were British soldiers inside who overheard. Coming out to investigate and realizing the situation, they motioned for me to come in. I wanted to bring Alem as well, since I was concerned for his safety and didn't want to lose his company. However, they wouldn't allow it, so before entering I turned to him to say goodbye with a full heart, telling him that God was watching over us. He shook my hand and we parted ways.

"Please keep in contact!" I shouted, and thought of the great debt that I owed my friend. He was a very good man.

Inside, I gave my passport to the receptionist, who must have had the most serene expression in all of Kabul. I was given a room key and the Wi-Fi password, which to my mind was obviously for goofing off, and was then escorted to my new quarters and told that I should change into Western clothes. With a sigh of relief, I walked into my new accommodation and realized that here in an unknown compound in Taliban-occupied Kabul, I again had a better room than my private student housing back at university. This was definitely becoming a trend, and I made a mental note to seriously reconsider my Western mode of living. After taking some time to change and allowing myself to feel comfortable for the first time that day, I went about the important business of logging into the Wi-Fi and doing a speed test. With a laugh, I realized that again it was better than what I had at home.

I decided to explore my room more thoroughly. The glass on the windows had to be at least three times thicker than standard. On the outside, there was a panel of lightly rusted metal with a latch. I tried it out and discovered that I had surely the best blackout curtain in the city. Looking

Inside the Turkish compound, in Western clothes again

out, I could just about see over the compound wall. The area was obscured by the dust kicked up from the nearby road by cars and smoke from some unseen nearby fire. Inside the room, I had a double bed with a firm mattress and a desk with a 32-inch TV hung above it. I turned on the air conditioning, and it made my room ice cold within minutes, a pleasant change from a day of racing through the heat. The bathroom felt modern and Western, with sterile white tiles, a large shower, and a non-cloggable toilet. The lights were warm and bright and activated by the key card, just as they would be in a normal Western hotel.

For a while I stayed in my room and used the time to gather as much information as I could from social media. I also messaged other people, such as the Polish woman I'd met earlier who had been on her way to parts remote. She apparently hadn't even realized the takeover of the country was going on until it was too late to act on it. I informed her that she was now certainly in Taliban territory. She seemed unfazed in response, which I greatly respected.

The green digital clock on the bedside stand read 8:03 p.m. The sun had set outside over the mountains, and the streets had gone almost totally silent. All the shops were shut tight, and no one wanted to venture outside. The majority of the Taliban were likewise inside celebrating, while essential soldiers patrolled the streets enforcing the new mandatory curfew. Cracking my window open slightly, I watched the black turban-clad conquers march to and fro for a while, trying to discern the pattern to their routine just in case it turned out that I needed to make a run for it. I had no desire to set out on my own, but I'd seen on the news that the Taliban had broken into some safehouses and chased out the Westerners hiding there.

My stomach rumbled, and I was reminded of the hunger tugging at the bottom of my gut. I went downstairs and headed into the canteen, where a few Western soldiers were hanging out. Two of them were playing a game of pool while others sat outside drinking and chatting. Their casual disposition helped set my mind somewhat at ease.

Not being too picky with food, I settled for a blackened banana from the dining area's display cabinet and went to sit outside on the porch to eat. After a few moments I feel a fluffy tail brush past. There were no furries in Kabul, not even at this Western safehouse. Confident in this, I turned and discovered a quite healthy-looking, black house cat looking for some attention, without a thought or care for the political developments affecting us humans. Glad for the company, I started stroking it, listening to its purr and watching it fold appreciatively into my lap. I'm allergic to cats, but the blocked nose and itchy eyes were a price I was happy to pay at the time for the benefit of my furry comrade's temporary company.

I headed back to my room and met a British soldier walking up the stairs to the next floor. We greeted each other, and he asked me what company I was there working for. I told him that I was actually here on a tourist visa doing some sightseeing and charity work. He roared with laughter.

"Fucking mental!" He waved me on. "Come up, have a drink, tell us some more."

I went up and was introduced to two other army lads from the British SAS. They all looked to be above the age of thirty and sported deep tans, meaning that it likely wasn't their first time in the graveyard of empires. They were snacking on the contents of their duffle bag—peanuts, Pringles, and alcohol—and offered me some, which I gladly accepted. I flinched initially at the bourbon since I don't drink due to seeing too many bad things done by alcohol to other people, but reflecting on the situation I decided in this case, why not. My first glass of alcohol in six years did take the edge off and helped me relax and fall into conversation. The soldiers were all tipsy and enjoying themselves and started telling me about what they'd experienced. It turned out they had been in a different safehouse earlier, which got overrun.

I nodded, recalling what I'd read online. "I heard on the news that the Taliban were doing that, trying to find Westerners hiding in safehouses."

"No, no! It's the locals," the soldier exclaimed, and went on after I looked at him in surprise. "Think about it. The banks have run dry, the sorry chaps are sure that they've lost their life savings. So, they take advantage of the chaos and start looting Western buildings. If anything, we were in more danger from them. They're not always very grateful."

"Were they threatening? How did you get out if they were trying to plunder your safehouse?"

Goofing off with the SAS

"We offered them cash; to them it's a small fortune," another soldier chimed in.

"So true. What has the situation been like in here?"

"There's been a lot of gunfire outside the walls, but we've been safe in here. At this point it's the Taliban curfew giving us peace, ironically."

We continued talking about my journey that day and they told me more about the situation at the airport. It's screwed long-term, they said. Each country was rushing in their troops as fast as they could, and intelligence indicated that it would quickly become a hotspot for ISIS-K and other groups unfriendly to the Taliban to target. I was very thankful at this point that I'd followed my gut and chosen not to stay there.

I went on to tell them about the rest of the time I'd spent in Afghanistan and how I took pictures with the Taliban earlier. They were laughing, and I could tell they weren't sure exactly how to react, but also couldn't get enough of my crazy story.

"You're an absolute legend," one of them said, shaking his head. "But you're also a bloody lunatic!"

They started giving me some practical tips for extreme survival while dressing me in their military gear. One of them handed me his black plate carrier vest. "Here, put this on."

I put on the body armor, which was weighed down by the magazines stored in the front pockets in addition to the plates. They also handed me a gun, after profuse warnings to keep my finger off the trigger since they didn't unload it. I handed one of them my phone and grinned as he snapped a picture to commemorate the occasion. They started talking me through the art of aiming properly, explaining in detail which eye to use, what the various parts of the gun were and how they worked, and other general tips. We bantered back and forth laughing like old friends. One of them went on a drunken rant about his sweater that was made out of merino wool and how well it had held up over the years, and how the prices had shot up. It seemed impressive, but despite lying about being Welsh, I didn't actually know anything about sheep or wool. They told me that this would be one of the most memorable trips of my life, which I had some inkling of already.

They told me a story about a legendary man on the Taliban side who had been through every Afghan war since the Soviets invaded, and his great-grandfather was rumored to have fought in the British war. They laughed while telling me I would need the body armor if I ever encountered him. He was very old with gray hair and unable to stand straight but had the blood of a young man and was well known in military circles as he would run up to American convoys during the occupation and try to stab the windows of the Humvees with his knife while screaming. He did not like any foreigner (based). However, he was ultimately harmless. The worst he would do is take a few swings at you with his fists, but whenever there were Americans around, he would attack their vehicles. They had learned to just leave him alone and let him take out his anger on their trucks.

After a while, they told me that they needed to get up at 5:00 a.m. to help some journalists stuck elsewhere in Kabul and that we should all get some sleep. Noticing that it was already 2:00 a.m. and they were all beyond tipsy, I thanked them for their time and headed to my room to rest in my own bed.

August 16th and 17th
A Long Night

THE WHOLE DAY OF AUGUST 16TH WAS MOSTLY UNEVENTFUL. I DIDN'T leave the compound all day. I would eat my meals, and other than that spent most of my time talking with the soldiers or checking my phone while waiting for any news of something happening outside or of us being allowed to leave. I spent a few moments in quiet prayer, thanking God for getting me safely thus far and asking His help to get me safely home.

There was one notable thing that did happen that day, which is that I got dumped. When I'd brought up the idea of the trip to Afghanistan to my girlfriend at the time, she'd thought it was a great idea, and for most of the time was very supportive. We had exchanged messages throughout the trip and I had sent her some pictures of myself having a grand old time. Rather abruptly from my perspective, I opened my phone to a WhatsApp message saying "I can't do this anymore."

The media had picked up my story by this point, and some of what they had to say wasn't very nice. They were calling me an idiot, saying that I was making light of the suffering of the Afghans, and implying that I was far right politically, which for the media at least is about the worst thing that can be said about someone. It apparently had really gotten to her, and who knows what else others around her were saying.

I tried to reassure her that it was fine and would all blow over, and that she should know better than to believe the media's sensationalist slanders. She was very worried that journalists would come after her and she would also get bad publicity and possibly have other issues in her personal or professional life, which I thought was somewhat silly as she wasn't on any of my social media and, for the most part, we'd kept our relationship very private. We'd hardly even told anyone we were dating. I asked if it could at least wait until I returned, since it wasn't a very nice feeling to deal with a breakup while I was preoccupied with trying to survive a war zone surrounded by the Taliban. I told her that if I didn't make it back then there wouldn't be an issue anyway. But despite my reassurances, she was adamant about breaking up and eventually just stopped responding.

I went to sleep that night newly single and feeling neither nearer nor farther from my goal.

The next day we all gathered in the courtyard of the compound in the morning. Most of the people there with us were foreign workers from Indonesia and the Philippines. I mostly stuck with the SAS guys. There were other military personnel who began shouting that we might be moving in a few hours and everyone should prepare themselves and any stuff they wanted to take with them. Each person was told they could only bring one bag that weighed no more than 22 lbs. People were queueing up with everyone trying to stay in the shade as the day was rapidly becoming as hot as ever.

The courtyard was bounded by walls about fifteen feet high, all topped with barbed wire. There were two or three soldiers who were focused on patrolling the area and staying alert to what was going on outside. The whole time, we heard frequent shots echoing in the air, even though we were near the airport. Evidently, they still hadn't completely calmed down.

People soon began sitting down. We were told by the military that the wait would only be a few hours. After around two or three hours with our exit seemingly no closer, we started realizing it would likely take longer, which was a consistent theme throughout the whole evacuation. Midway through the wait, some of the soldiers pulled out a crate of cold Sprite and started sharing it. I got one and grabbed a few more for the

SAS soldiers with whom I was still sitting. I then started shaking some and giving it to the Indonesian workers, who were surprised and shouted when it sprayed them, but laughed it off. Everyone was in high spirits.

There were some dogs resting in the sun. I wasn't sure exactly what they were, but they looked like some kind of spaniel. I got bored of looking at my phone after a while, so I went over and sat down next to them and started petting them, which they much appreciated. The SAS came over as well and told me that these were Springer Spaniels and they were military dogs.

"What's going to happen with them; are they coming with us?"

One of the SAS men shook his head. "No, the Taliban don't allow it."

"Why not?"

"They don't think of dogs as pets. In their religion, the dogs are *haram*, or forbidden. So they'll let us evacuate, but not with the dogs."

We talked about what was going to happen to the dogs and began contemplating if it would be more humane to shoot them, rather than let them starve on the streets of Afghanistan, be sold for meat, or be sold to China (also for meat). The SAS soldiers stroked the dogs to keep them calm and give them some comfort while they talked about the Taliban's cruelty.

"It's like a form of conquest," one of them commented. "They're taking our property from us to show that they're in control."

Fortunately, we eventually got some good news from the outside world. Someone had already made some calls, and an hour later we learned that a dog handler from the ANA had agreed to take them for a few hundred dollars, which the SAS gladly paid out of their pockets. It felt good to know that the dogs wouldn't be executed. Hopefully I could say the same for us soon.

At that moment we heard shouting, and the other military personnel conducting the evacuation began to get everyone lined up in order and ready to go. They announced that we would be crossing from the compound to the airport, which was just a short walk away. Everyone with weapons had to surrender them to the Taliban, with the promise that they would be returned once we crossed. We all got into a double-file line, and the SAS walked up and down telling everyone to "smile and wave, boys, smile and wave." I smirked remembering the line from *Madagascar.*

As the gates opened up, we saw a row of Taliban fighters surrounding the area with big smiles on their faces. These lads were clearly enjoying their victory. There were also other Afghans inside and outside. On the left, I saw a barbed wire fence with a section lifted up so that people could climb through. They were passing children through it, some that looked as young as one year old. There was some torn cloth on the fence, so it looked like someone had cut themselves on it, and I really hoped it wasn't a child.

The gates of the area we were in opened up into what looked like another, larger courtyard, about triple the size. At the end was another gate and wall where we could see more British soldiers perched on top. Some were just watching, while others were snipers in position, closely surveying everything that happened. That was where we had to get to, and the only thing that stood between us and freedom was a five-minute walk. But if something went wrong, we would have no defense. I watched one of the Taliban soldiers inspect one of the British soldier's service pistols. We'd also heard of recent ISIS-K bombings and knew that this was just the kind of area they would target, as indeed they later did.

On the right we saw a group of Afghans—men, women, and children—huddled in a circle. They looked beaten up, and I learned that these were people who had tried to escape or get into the airport without the Taliban's permission and had been caught. There was an old Taliban member guarding them. The SAS burst out laughing when they saw him and told me that he was none other than the same old war vet that they had told me about, the one who used to stab Humvees. He was pacing around the circle of people with a whip and randomly cracking it on the ground to keep them in place while yelling like a schizophrenic on speed. I doubted that any of the Afghans would try to get past him.

As we walked forward out of the compound, the Taliban were waving and smiling. Some of the fighters pointed at us and even took selfies. Every once in a while, we heard gunshots getting closer and closer. A plane flew directly above, and at that point we heard the whiz of bullets overhead no more than a few feet away from us.

"Get down!" Everyone dropped down in a panic, and I heard the SAS soldier next to me swearing under his breath. However, the Taliban quickly walked over and started reassuring us. One of them put a hand on my shoulder and explained that it was just the guy whose job it was to shoot into the air to indicate that a plane was landing. If he'd spoken better English, I would have told him how retarded that was. After waiting a few seconds and realizing that we all still had our heads on, we got back up and kept going.

We were told to walk very slowly. The Taliban fighters were thronging around us and kept smiling and saying things like, "it's all good," "you will go home very happy, very safe," and giving us thumbs up. At one point two of the younger Taliban who looked no older than twenty saw me, and when their eyes met mine, I could tell they recognized me. They must have known me due to my 4chan posts, which had by now hit Afghan social media as the story of the guy who came to Afghanistan as a tourist. They enthusiastically asked me for a selfie, pantomiming with their phones and motioning to make themselves understood. I looked to the SAS guy and he nodded that it was ok. Besides, I couldn't really have said no.

I put a smile on my face and let them each snap a pic. Somewhere out there is a selfie with me and those mad lads floating around. If anyone reading this happens to find those selfies, I'd love to see them.

We kept inching toward the main barrier between the Taliban side, where we were, and the British side beyond the wall. They had a list of names, and we were instructed to enter one at a time as we heard our name called. It was really funny to watch the British soldiers in their accents try to shout out Indonesian or Filipino names. One of the workers started helping after a while when they butchered the names too badly. Eventually they finished and there were some people left over whose names hadn't been called. The Taliban saw this and proclaimed that those people were Afghans trying to sneak out and dragged them away.

They called my name toward the end. The SAS soldiers had to wait for everyone to go through, and since I was British, they wanted to wait for me as well. They joked around that the British prime minister, Boris Johnson, must have had a file slapped on his desk with a picture of me and my 4chan posts saying that they needed to get me home for political reasons (the *Daily Mail* would've put out a hit piece otherwise).

We hurried our way to the section of the airport where the NATO evacuation was being processed. The area was packed, mostly with the Indonesian and Filipino foreign workers desperate to secure their place on the Western planes under any pretext. The babble of voices filling the air showed that most of these people didn't even speak English. They also clearly couldn't understand time-honored English traditions such as queueing, as I saw several of them pushing and shoving with soldiers who were trying to coax them into following an orderly process.

"Hey, let me see your bag." My attention pivoted to the no-nonsense-looking British soldier who gave me the order. We all complied and handed over our bags, which they tossed over to the side. The soldier stood on his guard in front of us while others rifled through our belongings. Satisfied, they returned our bags to us and we were waved through to immediately make our way to stand in line behind the Afghans trying to understand England's favorite pastime.

The tension in the room was palpable. I could certainly sympathize to an extent. The cloud of the Taliban still hung over us all, and everyone here must have felt like they were almost there, almost on the safe side, and maybe a bit of shoving and pushing was all that stood between them and freedom. Still, it was a frustrating atmosphere, and I could see the soldiers sighing as they looked at the sight before them. There were probably over two hundred people in that room being evacuated at that moment, and who knows how many would pass through over the course of the day.

Eventually we moved through the line to another security checkpoint. I was instructed to place my arms to the side and space my legs and then patted down.

"Clear, go over there please." We were directed to a waiting area, and another soldier stepped forward to escort us. His eyes widened and a smile cracked his lips as he saw me.

"Glad you made it out, Lord Miles." He placed a hand on my arm as we walked along and leaned in to whisper to me, "You're the 4chan kid, right?"

I didn't know that British soldiers browsed 4chan and also thought it was funny to be referred to that way. "Yes, that's me."

"The lads at the base are all following your story. We've been rooting for you to make it out alive."

Glad at the sentiment, though somewhat puzzled by the alternative, I spoke in a hoarse voice, "That's amazing. I didn't realize so many people knew."

Outside, we sat down on the dusty ground in front of a brick wall. Everyone was filed into seven rows with about thirty people in each. Around me, people munched on snacks and chocolate bars, and one guy had a dry packet of pot noodles with Han script on it. I have no idea how he obtained it, but it raised the curious possibility of the existence of a Kabul Chinatown.

The chatter quieted down suddenly in a wave as an officer stepped up to the front of the rows of people to make an announcement. He said that the evacuation was going to be slow and estimated that we would be out in less than eight hours. This sounded just fine to me, I figured, as I was already in line and there was not much more that I could do, and eight hours ultimately wasn't so long to wait. However, something told me that things might end up taking a bit longer than he'd promised.

We all got up again and started walking down the side of a dirt track roughly twenty or twenty-five feet wide, with large coils of barbed wire on either side running along sandy, beige brick and concrete walls with chipping paint. My nose took in the sharp smells of a construction site, and I realized that aside from that, the air felt a lot cleaner than downtown Kabul, with less fumes and general stuffiness.

I found myself walking alongside the guy with the pot noodles.

"You've got the right snack there, mate." He merely grunted in response. As we went along, he pulled out a second packet and started crunching on it like a chocolate bar, strolling as though without a care in the world. The dry brittle noodles must have gotten stuck in his throat, because he started coughing a bit suddenly, and I immediately pulled out a water bottle from the front storage of the beige body armor I'd been given that morning and offered it to him. He looked down at it with a look of slight disgust and without a word pulled out a Monster energy drink. I was very amused. If this man wasn't going to die from the Taliban, it seemed that he was on a mission to perish from his diet instead.

We carried on down the path for about twenty minutes. The scenery didn't really change, but I kept imagining that the plane would be around the corner any minute now. In my head I began to envision that this must be what a mouse trapped in a lab maze feels like while it's trying to find the cheese. Still, everyone was in high spirits. From behind me I heard some of the men singing. The pot noodle guy was playing the old "tap someone on the wrong shoulder to make them look the wrong way and then say hi from the other side" prank on his friends walking in front of him and laughing each time as though it were the funniest thing in the world. Mad respect to his goofy spirit. I started up a conversation with some of them and learned they were foreign workers in Afghanistan with a telecommunications company and most had been there about a year.

"I've only been here a week," another one chimed in. "I get here and next thing I know the Taliban are taking over the country!"

"You must be bad luck, mate," I told him, which got a laugh. They then started interrogating me.

"What company are you here with?"

"Oh, I'm not with a company. I'm here for tourism and charity."

They laughed even more. "Tourism?!"

"Yes, I got a tourist visa from the embassy in London, and I brought some money to give out to people in need."

"You're serious?"

"Yes, I can prove it to you if you want."

"So what have you been doing? Some kind of NGO or humanitarian work?"

"No, I've just been traveling and seeing the country and giving out the money that I had to people on the way." I told them about some of the adventures I'd had in the city and the country and meeting the Taliban.

The men were all enjoying my story immensely, shaking my hand and patting me on the back when hearing of my exploits. One of them congratulated me on being "big balled" and kindly handed me a can of 7 Up, which was still refreshingly ice cold.

Every once in a while, we saw a plane fly over, and it seemed like they were getting closer and closer to the ground as we continued on. I couldn't estimate how far away from the landing strip that put us, but it seemed within reach. I'd lost track of time entirely, and the memory of the compound I'd been in earlier felt like a different day.

Part of the crowd was a group of Indonesian lads, and as the planes got closer, I saw them pull out the calculators on their phones and start doing some kind of trigonometric calculations. They were all babbling in their incomprehensible native language, and as it got more intense, I felt a debate was breaking out. I asked one of my new friends who was staying quiet what it was about.

"They're trying to figure out how many miles away the plane is based on angle of descent and so on. But they're getting different answers from their estimations and so now they're complaining."

He listened some more and started chuckling. "They're comparing the rank and reputation of their engineering universities and arguing about how their superior school makes them right."

I laughed and contemplated suggesting to them that they simply average the two results, just to piss them off, but held back because I decided it would be more entertaining to see how they settled this. My friend continued interpreting to me quietly, and after a while they seemed to have come to an agreement.

"They've concluded that we shouldn't wonder how far the plane is or God may shoot it down and then we will have the plane too close to us."

I saw them all nodding as though their conclusion made perfect sense, and it made me wonder whether these weren't actually philosophy students, because that discussion was so outstanding and otherworldly.

I tapered off from that conversation to walk up and say hi to some of the British soldiers who asked me how I was doing.

"I'm quite enjoying myself, honestly," I replied, to which they looked pleased but cautioned that it was probably going to be a long night. I tried to pry more information out of them about what to expect, but with resigned smiles they indicated they had no idea what was going on themselves.

Walking behind the soldiers

After a while we stopped without having arrived anywhere that really looked like a destination. The soldier at the front of the line got our attention and said that we were going to be waiting here for a few hours. I realized that it was now evening. The sun had set and long shadows were crawling out across the sandy, hot ground. There were flood lights behind the wall on one side, which created a lot of shade on the path. I sat down without hesitation and adjusted my helmet, loosening the straps and tilting it so I could use it as a pillow while keeping it on. The body armor I wore was probably unnecessary by this point—the SAS had given it to me for the evacuation before we'd left the compound—but I found it to be really comfortable, almost like a weighted blanket. I laid down and felt the lukewarm temperature of the dusty road.

Me in my comfortable helmet

The chatter around me slowly began to calm down to an ambient level that I could ignore. Above, the stars were coming out. There was very little light pollution, and I saw the sky fill with brilliant twinkling sparks like I had never seen before. It was mystical, and out of everything I'd been through, this was the best moment.

I placed a facemask I'd been given over my eyes to make it easier to sleep and smoothly dozed off for a good hour or two, before being woken up by the sound of a convoy of armored vehicles rumbling past. I looked up to see some people shoot to their feet, thinking this was a transport for us, but unfortunately it carried on. Everyone eventually relaxed back into silence, but I could hear their thoughts of disappointment. Some people went back to sleep. I lay back down and put in my AirPods to listen to "Walking on Sunshine" by Katrina And The Waves while admiring the stars.

I found a YouTube video about Afghanistan tourism in my downloaded playlist and started watching it to get some retroactive advice on what I should have done. It opened by saying that while lots of the country was dangerous due to the war, Kabul was safe from the Taliban, and I chuckled at the irony of seeing that this had been posted only two weeks ago.

At that moment the soldiers at the front got up and started rousing people, telling us to start moving again. I tapped and shook some people sleeping around me to help us all get going, and we continued onward again.

At this stage we would walk, stop for around ten minutes and wait, walk again, then stop again, without any explanation given as to why. I was looking at my phone, and it struck me that I got 4G throughout most of Kabul, but not here, and I asked some of the guys around me if they had a phone signal. Everyone was having the same issue, getting either zero bars or just very weak 3G. We put two and two together when we noticed the multiple large antennas on each car that was passing by. As they drove past, everyone's signal became nonexistent, then when they were gone a few minutes later some people got a weak signal. There was a chance that mobile phones were being blocked by some military equipment, which would make sense considering the suicide bombings that had been taking place by the terrorist group ISIS-K around the country. I uploaded some updates to social media as we walked along and hoped that they would be posted later.

At around 10:00 p.m. we reached a gate with patches of grass surrounding it, which was a welcome change of terrain from the past few hours of only dirty, dusty, yellow and gray roads and crumbling concrete walls. With renewed energy, everyone eagerly broke formation and started jogging toward the front, pushing one another out of the way. I was in no rush and didn't want to let my emotions get the better of me. The way I saw it, we were all going to end up on the same plane that would depart at the same time, and anyway I considered the floor much more comfortable than economy class seats. I joked to myself in my head that perhaps the American Express staff were still in the airport and I could use my credit card to get into the business lounge to wait for my evacuation. I had also heard rumors on social media about a Kabul McDonalds, so I was half-hopeful that an alert would pop up on my Uber Eats app at any moment.

We were instructed to sit down again, which we all did. I stayed near the back and sat on a grassy mound that allowed me to peer over the fence. On the other side I saw soldiers scurrying to and fro under the wash of floodlights, with men loading and unloading supplies, people walking around with clipboards, and nobody eating dried pot noodles.

After a while I realized I needed to use the bathroom. I looked around, but there was no sign that we had been provided with even a portaloo, and as far as I knew we could be told to move again at any minute, so I didn't want to wander off looking. Not seeing any other option, I just walked over to the corner where the wall met the fence and started pissing. A few people glanced over, so to break the ice I pointed to the spot on the grass where I was peeing and said, "Taliban," which was rewarded with laughter. I finished and returned to occupy my throne of grass, rubble, and dust, only to see four or five other people get up and use the same newly found pissing corner. I'm willing to bet that that was the most watered chunk of grass in Afghanistan that day.

After about another twenty minutes of waiting for further direction, we finally got the announcement. Four of the soldiers from the front of our group got everyone's attention.

"Listen up! We will not be flying out tonight." The crowd groaned, but the soldiers ignored it. "We have temporary housing prepared; you are all going to spend the night there. You're going to be transported in cars; we can take ten of you at a time. Please line up in an orderly fashion, and we will select groups going from front to back. Everyone will be transported tonight; no one is going to stay here."

So much for eight hours, I thought. I also remembered how disorderly these people had been the last time that they had been told to queue. Sure enough, a crowd quickly formed with people trying to swamp the few soldiers controlling the operation. The first car rolled up, and before a group could be selected, something like forty people all just started walking toward it.

"Whoa, whoa!!" The officer and the other soldiers put out their arms to arrest the group's progress. "Whoever I pick goes; everyone else waits!"

The workers didn't understand this, or just weren't having it, and started gesturing and speaking angrily. The soldiers would very clearly point to one person to select him to go to the car, and four others surrounding him would also start walking. The soldiers were clearly getting impatient and frustrated and kept yelling at them all to get back in line, just for the process to repeat again.

I was sitting calmly in the back watching all this unfold, just sad that I didn't have a tub of popcorn at hand to help enjoy the show. The soldiers who were at the compound were to the side of me, laughing and placing bets with each other on how many times the instructions would have to be repeated. By that point it was over five, and I think they all lost.

It was pretty funny, but I also started getting annoyed as it really seemed that we were getting nowhere for at least ten or fifteen minutes now. I didn't understand why the foreign workers kept rushing and disregarding the instructions if they could see that it was just slowing down the process. The SAS lads were also running out of patience. They stated that they don't have a say in this, but they're just trying to get to bed soon, so they stepped off to the side in a clearly defined group and pulled me with them. We stood there quiet and orderly, and I felt like I was back at school and the teacher was picking who gets to go to recess first. Two other groups went ahead of us, and then we were picked to go in the next car. The officer up front made a point of using us as an example of proper behavior that gets rewarded. Now I really felt like this was a school experience.

We piled into the car and squeezed in, with people sitting on top of their luggage, bodies overlapping each other, and backpacks crammed into every bit of space inside. When we hit a bump, all of our heads hit the ceiling, and we all swayed back and forth in one mass together with every twist and turn and pothole in the uneven road.

One of the military lads squeezed my shoulder. "Are you doing alright, mate?"

"Oh, I'm fine," I smiled.

"Not exactly how you were expecting to leave the country, is it?"

"No, but I'd say things are going quite well."

They laughed good-naturedly. "That's a good attitude."

"He's a damn psychopath," another added, chuckling.

After a few minutes of driving, we pulled up to a structure that resembled several temporary school buildings fused into one urban jungle. There were lights on inside and people standing around. We piled out of the car and were instructed to put our belongings off to the side and wait again, so I looked up engrossed in further stargazing before a large man, who I guessed was Mongolian, handed me one of several coconut protein drinks that he was passing out. He wore a sweater that said "Kabul powerlifting," and his build confirmed it. I thanked him for the drink and realized that it tasted terrible, but I appreciated that I was in no situation to complain. Besides, I'm generally the type of person to eat almost any food I'm given, and this situation was no exception.

"Hey mate, give us a hand organizing this." The SAS were digging through the luggage, and I gladly assisted. They asked me to watch their stuff for them, which was the least I could do.

However, a fresh disappointment awaited us. After thirty minutes of waiting outside the building while other groups came to join us, we were all told that someone messed up and this was not where we were sleeping tonight. Another car soon pulled up to transport us, so we grabbed all our bags again and stuffed them in the trunk.

This time the drive was only a brief five minutes before we arrived at our final destination. It was very similar to the previous place, a walled compound that looked like much of it was still mid construction. Inside on the left were around eight temporary buildings all in one complex, and to the right were park benches with scraggly patches of grass surrounding them. Most of the buildings had cold, dim lights inside that felt like those of a corporate office. Near the entrance was one single-story, gray, rectangular building with stacks of supplies in and around it. The lights inside were much warmer.

I followed the SAS men and some of the workers into the building on the right. Inside we found piles of MREs in large cardboard boxes. I knew that it would be good to keep my stomach topped up at this point, as who knows when I would have the chance to eat again.

"Miles, you know we don't have any hot water to make that with; you might not want to eat it dry."

"That's a nonsense attitude."

The soldier laughed. "Suit yourself."

I dug into the MRE, which was pulled pork. In taste and texture, it was more like the dusty end part of a packet of bacon-flavored crisps, but it was good. There was a dog inside with us sitting down tied to a pipe, and I recognized it as the same as the spaniels from earlier. I poured some water from my bottle into my cupped hand and let him lap it up. He looked happy and not at all abused or distressed, so I didn't feel bad about us leaving him there. We sat on a bench to eat, and one of the workers gagged on the tuna meal he'd picked up from the MRE pile, so I swapped with him just because I wanted to try it. I don't know what he was complaining about, because it was great, better than most of the food I used to eat as a student.

After eating we were assigned buildings for the night. I was put together with one of the SAS guys. He warned me that the building wouldn't be very pretty, but when we got there, I saw that it had carpeted floor and working temperature control. It was very small, roughly eleven feet by fifteen, with an empty metal bed frame in one corner below a window that had a flood light outside shining directly through. The walls were damp, and the bathroom toilet neither flushed nor even had water inside. The shower seemed only half-built and had a hole in the ground, and the taps didn't work either. I pissed inside the shower hole and washed my hands with some wipes I had. We both joked that if either one of us snored that we should slap the other one awake.

The SAS soldier stated that I was taking our conditions surprisingly well, so I briefly explained that this room was bigger than my student room and told him about my time being homeless years ago. It wasn't hard to make me happy. He told me that in that case I should consider joining the army. I made a mental note to consider it given how much fun I was having.

I reflected back upon how well I slept while napping on the dirt road a few hours earlier. I'd woken up from that feeling great and actually well rested. When at home in England, I would exhaust myself working fourteen hours a day on a pitch deck with my investment banking job or university work but was never able to sleep without an hour of feeling like my time was being wasted or I hadn't done enough that day.

We both huddled in separate corners with our faces turned away from the beam of light coming through the window. I laid down on my side, planning to sleep in the body armor again because of how comfortable it was last time. We talked briefly about how the Taliban were able to take over the country so quickly, the fall of Kabul catching every government, news company, and ourselves off guard, and why every war analyst had been wrong. I learned from him that most of the Western-backed Afghan forces weren't paid consistently or sometimes at all, diminishing their loyalty. The Taliban were very effective at using social media to show their victories, which lowered the morale of the Afghans further. Air superiority was meant to be the game changer for the West, but when the US withdrew, they took all their knowledge about repairing and maintaining the aircrafts, which left the locals with little defense. Clearly both the competency and morale of the ANA had left much to be desired, even after twenty years.

About ten minutes into our conversation, we were startled by a banging on the door. Surprise, surprise, we're not staying here either. We both bounced to our feet immediately and went outside to see everyone else getting ready as well. I looked at my watch and saw that by now it was around 1:30 a. m. The time at this point felt very weird; the day had gone by so quickly, but at the same time so much had been happening that I felt like the trip had taken weeks. We huddled back into another car that banged against its suspension stops with no shock absorbers. One person next to me micro-slept in the back seat while drooling until the bumps in the road woke him up to us giggling at the sight.

We soon reached another location where we lined up to walk again. I was near the front behind two tall male soldiers, and there were about a hundred people in the group behind me. I could hear distant laughter and talking with everyone nearly stepping in unison. People were so desperate to get out that they didn't leave any spaces in the line for someone to overtake them. To the right was a battered concrete wall with barbed wire and to the left a continuous mound of dust, rubble, and dirt. The sky above was dark and empty now, with the stars drowned out by the glare of floodlights. Still, it seemed like maybe we were finally getting somewhere, because the area we were in now had a lot of activity. We saw more planes flying nearer and nearer. Some of the men amused themselves by pointing at the passing aircrafts and talking about which seat they wanted.

One of the SAS guys jogged up to me.

"Hey Miles, how are you holding up? Are you doing alright?"

"Oh, it's great, thank you! I'm glad to be here."

He looked a bit shocked at the contrast between my high spirits and the situation I was in, but at this point wasn't too surprised. He tapped one of the soldiers leading the line and pointed back at me.

"This lunatic is here on holiday; did you know that? I told him if this is his idea of a holiday, he should join the army."

The two soldiers looked at each other and laughed.

"He's got balls 'en, don't he," one of them said. They agreed with the SAS guy that I was a lunatic, but it was all in good fun. I conversed by sharing some of the photos of me operating the turreted machine gun on the Taliban vehicle, which they took in with absolute amazement at my daring and the fact that I wasn't dead. In return they shared stories they'd heard about a Polish woman who was cycling through the Middle East and was currently trapped in Kandahar by the Taliban advance. I was astonished, as there was no doubt that this was the very same woman I'd met days ago. It made me a bit worried for her safety, but there was nothing I could do, and I was reassured by the fact that the military knew about her situation.

We reached another queue. There were about thirty people in front of me. We were approached by an elderly gentleman in uniform who stated that we had to remove all liquids, creams, deodorant, food, and razors, and make sure that our bags were below 22 lbs. Additionally, only backpacks were allowed. We'd originally been under the impression that we could also bring additional luggage, like a suitcase, thinking that perhaps they would be stowed separately. Now it appeared that the only things we would be taking with us would be what fit on our backs. It quickly became a scramble as the few hundred people who spoke poor English tried to prioritize their belongings. I communicated the information to some of the better English speakers who then passed it down the line in other languages. I assumed that the body armor would be taken off me; however, I also wondered if I'd be able to keep it if I just acted confidently enough. After all, very few people seemed to know what was actually going on, so it was worth a shot. Plus, holding onto it might be useful just in case something did happen; after all, we were still in Afghanistan.

Everyone had the same idea of spraying the entirety of their aftershave onto themselves before tossing it away, becoming more flammable than Thích Quảng. There were no plastic bags or bins to dump your stuff in, so everyone just decided on one designated pile. A lot of people got rid of secondary shoes, hats, and clothes, but there were also some oddi-ties such as a tiger teddy bear, which made me suspicious that there might be a Reddit furry among us as I hadn't seen anyone younger than twenty so it couldn't have been a kid's. Another weird one was an almost empty large bottle of vodka, but I didn't see any potential Russians or Irish in the line. The worst one, or perhaps best, was an alarm clock shaped like a cartoon bomb. I picked it up and showed it to some people around me, who jumped initially. We cackled at how this could have got-ten past security without a check.

As some people tossed out food, the rest of us saw an opportunity for a free meal and began eating whatever chocolates or other sweets we could find. I found a small bottle of high-quality Canadian maple syrup, which I downed over the course of under a minute. A few Indonesian men had the genius idea of filling my body armor with food, and people

The maple syrup I chugged

began stuffing my backpack and the pockets alongside my helmet with protein bars. I probably had thirty protein bars on me in total. Their reasoning was that I had packed lightly and my body armor meant that I could sneak things through, and in any case, it seemed better than leaving it all to the pile.

In front of us was a large building, and as the line approached the entrance, I was able to peer inside. On the left was a scale and a female soldier in her mid-twenties sitting at a desk checking people in. I observed one man's bag weigh in at 26 lbs., just over the limit, and he was told he needed to lose some items, so he went back out to sacrifice to the pile. The next man walked up to be registered, and his bag weighed 22.5 lbs., but he was turned away because he had a second bag, which wasn't allowed. The one after that was even worse; his bag was over 33 lbs. He tried using the scale multiple times and didn't seem to understand, or want to accept, that it was simply overweight. He had a hiking backpack that looked quite empty, so whatever he had in it must have been dense. On the outside was what looked like a lightweight, foam sleeping mat. The army lady took off the plastic, black bin bag it was wrapped in to discover a tightly packed, large, Afghan rug. Caught red-handed, the man reluctantly abandoned the rug and managed to continue into the building with the weight reduction.

I was next, and when I walked in the lady smiled at me, pleasantly surprised to see a Western face. I showed her my passport and stated my name. When she asked which business I was with, I asked her to look at the visa on my passport.

"A tourism visa, that's a first! Welcome back, Miles." She flashed me a lovely, genuine smile.

I placed my backpack on the scale with a drumroll playing in my head, only to see it reach just above 11 lbs. Everyone behind me started laughing.

"You're making my job a lot easier," the soldier chuckled. I asked her about the arsenal of protein bars stashed on my person, and she said quietly that I should be fine. I handed her one in thanks and walked off smiling to myself. I was still the protein bar man.

Next up was another female soldier with a small Springer Spaniel that was acting as a sniffer dog. However, I noticed that the dog was very distracted and needed to be bribed with treats every time he was supposed to sniff something. Everyone had to place their items on the floor, and the dog would do a loop around the bag, which only took a moment. It didn't seem like the most effective security measure.

She recognized me as I approached and told me that the soldiers had been staying updated on my story. She found it hilarious. I set my bag down for the dog to begin his work.

"He seems very distracted."

She sighed heavily. "I know. Sniffer dogs really shouldn't be expected to sniff three hundred bags in a row. He just keeps getting more and more distracted and I have to keep giving him treats, which makes him start treating it like a game and giving false positives just to get another one. What should have happened is for everyone to put their bags down together in one pile and have the dog sniff them all at once."

My bag passed somehow, and I handed her a protein bar. She was surprised but took it gratefully. I could tell she had a long night left, and it was the least I could do. She was very playful with the dog, and it was cute to see the close connection they seemed to have.

The next room contained the third and final checkpoint, which just involved a bag search. Two soldiers started looking through my bag as another one checked my passport. He glanced up and asked if I was the lad online who went to Afghanistan on holiday. When I told them I was, their eyes lit up and they each asked for a photo of me to send to their mates back home, then shook my hand as I walked to the waiting room.

We were all asked to wait in one of four identical rooms. They were nearly empty with only one chair, so everyone laid on the floor to relax, and a few people slept. I started handing out protein bars, and despite the language barrier between myself and the workers, we soon became friends. For a while, I watched the dog from the door frame for entertainment while listening to a Beastie Boys playlist through my AirPods.

After half an hour or so everyone was herded into another room deeper into the building. We all picked up our bags, presuming that this would finally be the entrance to our flight, but that again wasn't the case. Instead, it turned out to be a hall with a muddy, blue vinyl flood and some school-style lunch tables. The staff informed me that we might have to spend another day or two there waiting, which was fine with me.

We laid down on the floor once again, fitting our bodies together next to each other like a game of Tetris. There was hardly enough room for an inch of personal space. By now it was almost 4:00 a.m., my stomach was full of protein bars, and I'd begun crashing from the maple syrup high. Within minutes, I slumped unconscious with a mask over my face and my helmet as a pillow. I fell asleep knowing I was closer to finally flying out.

August 18th
Evacuation

I WOKE UP TO NAMES BEING SHOUTED OUT. I WAS SOMEWHAT DEFLATED from sleeping with the heavy body armor on. Level 3 plates are comfortable when you want a weighted blanket, but they also compress your muscles and joints while you're sleeping for any extended time. I stumbled to my feet and listened closely to hear my name. I laughed in my head at hearing some British soldier once again butchering Indonesian names. After twenty minutes or so of watching everyone around me get called, pack up their stuff, and walk off, the list came to an end. I almost got excited at the thought that I might be spending more time in Afghanistan, but I was really feeling the need for a shower and a fresh pair of socks by then.

I approached the staff.

"Hey, I didn't hear my name on the list. It's Miles Routledge; do you have me on there or do I have to stay here?"

They laughed. "Don't worry Miles. The list is mainly to keep Afghans from sneaking in. You can go ahead to the plane as well; no one will stop you."

I went outside and joined the rest. I had to squint as the bright sunlight blinded my eyes. The heat was as blistering as ever, and as we walked toward the runway, I could feel it burning my feet up through my cheap shoes.

As we stood around waiting, I saw a group of British soldiers glance over and take notice of me. Some of the young lads started smiling and gave me a thumbs up. I could tell they definitely knew who I was from my 4chan posts. My story had been passed around all the army chats by that point, and I was something of a living myth for them. They were really enthused to see me, and a few came up to ask for selfies, pat me on the back, and express congratulations or encouragement.

"Good on you!"

"So glad you made it!"

"See you next war!"

Boarding the plane

I took that last one as a personal invitation to any upcoming conflicts, so thank you for that, soldier lads. I had one senior officer approach and ask if I was the kid with the tourist visa for Afghanistan.

"Yes," I replied simply, and he stared back with the most dumb-founded expression I'd ever seen, while the staff around him continued smiling at me and giving thumbs up. There seemed to be a clear divide between the opinions of the younger and the older generations in the army.

We were escorted to a big UK Royal Air Force plane starting up on the runway. The spinning turbines provided a welcome breeze as we queued up to enter. People rushed to be first in line, but I realized those first in would reside at the back, whereas if I was at the front I might have a view, plus I would get off the plane first. They announced that the plane was headed to an airfield near Swindon, England after a layover in Dubai, and everyone was going regardless of nationality, which made the Indo-nesians cheer. The army tried to load the aircraft ten people at a time, but many wouldn't listen and tried to sneak in early before getting pushed back by a soldier who could count. I had learned by this point that civil-ians must be a major pain for the military during these types of situa-tions.

Upon entering, we realized there were no seats as the interior was stripped to a bare minimum and contained only the safety equipment and netting on the cold gray walls alongside the clips for cargo on the floor. There was not a single Afghan on the plane, which at least meant I wasn't taking anyone's spot as this plane wasn't being used to evacuate Afghan refugees. The incidents where people clung to the outside of planes and fell off happened at another runway.

Most people inside crossed their legs, but to me this was unbearable after years of leg day without any regular stretching routine. I felt more stress from leg cramps than I did from the fall of Kabul. The plane rum-bled, and we felt it start to move, picking up speed down the runway. Takeoff was rough, but the commanding officer and pilot made it fun to distract us by acting as though it were a civilian aircraft, telling us that unfortunately there wouldn't be any champagne on this flight. People were chuckling and overall everyone was still in excellent spirits.

When we reached a steady altitude, I said *screw it* to myself and stood up to relieve my legs, with many people immediately following my example. It got a bit weird for a moment when about two hundred people all stood up over the course of a minute and the officers didn't seem to know whether they should allow it. Most soon sat back down though. Many of the army lads at the front laid down and slept, and I think they certainly needed it. Flights always make me sleepy, and I soon began involuntarily micro-sleeping while standing up, which was a very dangerous combination, because if I fell over, I'd probably nutcracker some poor Indonesian guy's skull with my helmet. I decided to listen to the *Doom* soundtrack on max volume on repeat through my AirPods to help me stay awake. I didn't have any room to take off my body armor, so I ended up looking like a psychotic war junkie blasting action music, all kitted out with eyes twitching. I stood for the entire three-hour flight to Dubai and did not regret it. My legs felt great whereas others fell over while trying to stand up after landing because their feet had fallen asleep or cramped.

Inside the plane to Dubai

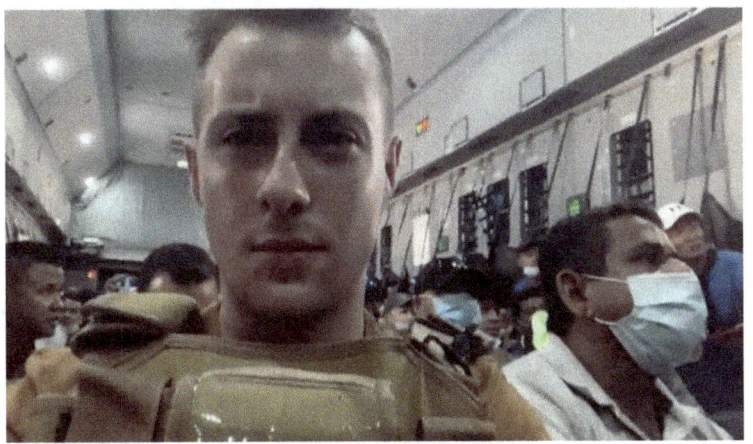

Me on the plane to Dubai

In Dubai, we walked out to behold a sea of temporary accommodations set up, with tents and basic bedding. I fully expected to spend at least a night here, and it seemed like the staff did too. I heard them joking about how they're working this shift on the shortest of notices and were not sure what to make of it. They showed us how to connect to the Wi-Fi, but with hundreds trying at once it simply crashed and didn't work. Sadly, I could not shitpost in Dubai.

I took my body armor off to walk through the security checkpoint. The staff there glanced at me and asked if I was allowed to have that. I really wanted to keep it, so I paused and simply said, "Yes," flashing the keycard that I still had for the Turkish compound, which they took as some kind of position of authority and let me carry on. Free body armor secured!

I was really hungry at that point, and luckily, I was almost immediately offered a sandwich and crisps; however, I noticed a vegan sticker on them and had to turn them down. I'd rather go hungry for a few hours than take estrogen snacks.

People started to lay down and prepare themselves for a long stay; however, only a few minutes later we were told to line up as we were boarding for Swindon. This was a confusing but very welcome surprise, as now I wouldn't have to discover how many people in this huge area snored. I glanced around to spot the people with weak jawlines. I glared at them, guessing they snored. I had come to associate mouth breathing with a convex face.

My sleep deprivation really hit at this point, and I'm fuzzy on further details. The RAF aircraft that took us to Swindon was much more comfortable than the previous one, with padded seating and lots of legroom. As far as I was concerned, it topped first class on a normal plane. After takeoff, the lights dimmed, and I finally slept soundly before waking up to a smooth landing. I looked out a window to my left to see green fields and dreary skies.

I had made it back to England.

Postscript

I returned to Afghanistan again in 2022. I'd originally made plans to help my former tour guide, Alem, get out of the country, as he was afraid of reprisals due to having worked for the US occupation. He had been of inestimable value to me, and without him the trip wouldn't have been anywhere near as exciting, and I may well have never made it back. However, this plan unfortunately fell through as he went back on his end of it at the last minute. Not to waste the trip, I spent the time catching up with the Taliban instead, going shooting, having tea, and going on Afghan TV. Perhaps you'll read about it in a future book.

Until then, God bless,
LORD MILES

Additional Pictures

Outside the airport in Kabul

Driving through Kabul

Inside a restaurant I visited

More Afghan food

I bought this to give to my then-girlfriend on the second day at one of the market stands on the side of the road. They charged me a whole $2!

A picture I took on our way up north on the second day

A view of Kabul

This was a cemetery for Western soldiers who fought in Afghanistan that we stopped at on the second day. Some of them were from as far back as the British war.

A selfie after reaching the Turkish compound

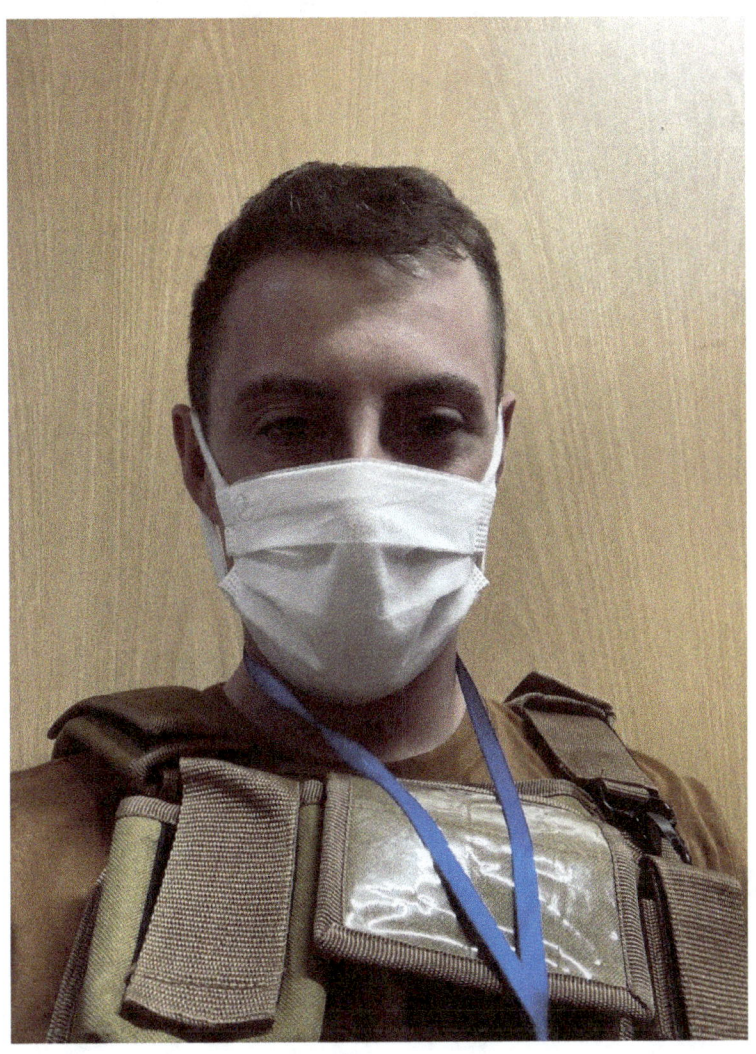

Another picture from evacuation day